RATHER DIE
FIGHTING

Europe 1937

- - - International borders of 1937

SWEDEN

Baltic Sea

Riga

LATVIA

LITHUANIA

North Sea

DENMARK

Copenhagen

Danzig

EAST PRUSSIA

Bialystok

SCHLESWIG-HOLSTEIN

Hamburg

Stettin

Treblinka

Warsaw

POLAND

HOLLAND

Berlin

GERMANY

Lublin

Majdanek

Breslau

Kattowice

Cracow

Frankfurt-on-Main

Prague

Auschwitz

Zeilsheim

CZECHOSLOVAKIA

FRANCE

Stuttgart

Vienna

Budapest

AUSTRIA

HUNGARY

ROMANIA

Zurich

SWITZERLAND

YUGOSLAVIA

Milan

Trieste

ITALY

Adriatic Sea

Mediterranean Sea

| 0 | kilometres | 300 |
| 0 | miles | 200 |

© Martin Gilbert 2009

RATHER DIE FIGHTING

A MEMOIR OF WORLD WAR II

FRANK BLAICHMAN

INTRODUCTION AND MAPS BY SIR MARTIN GILBERT

Arcade Publishing   New York

Arcade Publishing books may be purchased in bulk at special discounts
for sales promotion, corporate gifts, fund-raising, or educational purposes.
Special editions can also be created to specifications. For details, contact the
Special Sales Department, Arcade Publishing, 307 West 36th Street, 11th
Floor, New York, NY 10018 or info@skyhorsepublishing.com.

Arcade Publishing® is a registered trademark of Skyhorse Publishing, Inc.®,
a Delaware corporation.

www.skyhorsepublishing.com

10 9 8 7 6 5 4 3 2 1

Library of Congress Cataloging-in-Publication Data

Blaichman, Frank.
  Rather die fighting : a memoir of World War II / Frank Blaichman ;
inroduction and maps by Martin Gilbert.
      p. cm.
  Originally published: 2009.
  Includes bibliographical references and index.
  ISBN 978-1-61145-015-6 (pbk. : alk. paper)
  1. Blaichman, Frank. 2. Jews--Poland--Biography. 3. World War,
1939-1945--Poland--Personal narratives, Jewish. 4. World War,
1939-1945--Jewish resistance--Poland--Personal narratives. 5. Holocaust,
Jewish (1939-1945)--Poland--Biography. 6. Poland--Biography. I. Title.
  DS134.72.B55A3 2011
  940.53'18092--dc22
  [B]
                                                    2011001615

Printed in the United States of America

For my parents, brothers, and sisters,
who died decades before their time.

And for Cesia, who has given me a good life,
and for my children and grandchildren.

Central Poland

River Vistula

River Bug

Treblinka

Warsaw

Radzyn

Parczew

Serock

Lubartow

Wlodawa

Sobibor

Radom

Pulawy

Markuszow

Lublin

Majdanek

River Wieprz

Skarzysko-Kamienna

Bystrzejowice

Chelm

Kielce

Janow

Pinczow

River Vistula

River San

Auschwitz

Cracow

0   kilometres   50

0   miles   30

© Martin Gilbert 2009

Between Parczew and Wlodawa

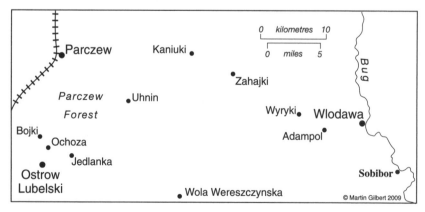

Parczew

Kaniuki

0   kilometres   10

0   miles   5

Zahajki

Bug

Parczew
Forest

Uhnin

Wyryki

Wlodawa

Bojki

Adampol

Ochoza

Jedlanka

Ostrow
Lubelski

Sobibor

Wola Wereszczynska

© Martin Gilbert 2009

CONTENTS

INTRODUCTION

IT IS AN HONOR TO WRITE a few words of introduction to this exceptional memoir. The Holocaust was on such a vast scale that no amount of published recollections by survivors could ever tell the complete story. Each memoir adds an important element: an aspect of the narrative, an account of survival, a testimony to human suffering and endurance.

In this memoir, we learn a great deal about one of the neglected aspects of the Jewish experience during the Second World War: the acts of resistance carried out by those who found the means, and the will, to challenge the mighty German war machine and apparatus of destruction.

Frank Blaichman commanded a Jewish partisan platoon. These seven words, so simple, and at the same time so unusual, mask a story of drama and danger, a story of which the Jewish people can be proud.

I was fortunate to have traveled in the early 1980s in the regions where the action in this book takes place. While researching my book *The Holocaust: The Jewish Tragedy*, I went to Frank Blaichman's hometown of Kamionka—twelve miles north of the Polish city of Lublin—and explored the forests where he had fought. In my *Atlas of the Holocaust*, I mapped many of the villages and woods where the action in this book takes place. I went deep into the forest, and found the remnants of some of the camps the author describes; I also sensed the hostility—surviving to this day—of the local population to the Jews who had refused to accept deportation and death.

Frank Blaichman was sixteen years old when war broke out in 1939, with the German invasion of Poland. His first sight of war was the influx of Jewish refugees from Warsaw, which had been savagely bombed. Then came Polish soldiers, in full retreat. Shortly after German soldiers reached Kamionka, a group of local Hasidim was rounded up, given shovels, and made to dig ditches. Frank writes, "As the Hasidim dug, the soldiers beat them with their rifle butts and made fun of them, cursing them, laughing at them when they fell. When the Hasidim finished digging the ditches, the soldiers made them fill them in again and went on beating them. I watched from a distance, shaken, and fantasized about taking revenge."

A teenager's fantasy was to become reality within three years. In September 1942, the Germans said they were going to move the Jews of Kamionka to nearby Lubartow, where a ghetto would be set up for all the Jews of the region. This promise of safety was a typical Nazi deception.

On the afternoon of October 8, 1942, it was learned that the deportation would take place the next day. Frank decided to escape—a decision that led, ultimately, to his becoming a Jewish partisan. The greater portion of his gripping memoir is the story of his two years in the forest. Told with meticulous detail and powerful emotion, it deserves to become a classic account of Jewish resistance.

"Skinny Frank," as he was known, had many brushes with the harsh reality of life in hiding in an occupied and hostile countryside. The Germans were a formidable and cruel adversary. On one occasion, after investigating the sound of German voices some way off, Frank and the small group with him returned to find that their underground bunkers had been attacked and everyone in them killed, seventy-five in all: "We swore that we would avenge the deaths of our comrades." The group was reduced in number to twenty-five. But it never gave up. Among the enemies it faced were Polish collaborators, eager for the money the Germans would pay for each Jew betrayed. Those collaborators who were caught by the group were executed. The local population had to learn that the killing of Jews would not go unavenged.

Some Polish farmers were glad to help; they, too, were under occupation. Polish partisans of the People's Guard (later the Armia Ludowa, or People's Army) welcomed the Jewish partisans as fellow fighters, while allowing them to remain an independent Jewish group and to continue to protect Jews in hiding.

Each of the partisan missions described here is full of danger and drama. Each adds to our knowledge of what was achieved by these small groups of Jewish fighters. Each is a tribute to remarkable courage and endurance.

Disappointment and success, help and betrayal, went hand in hand. Death stalked the daily life of the brave youngsters who had become soldiers without an army, without an arsenal, and without the support of the local population. But they persevered. The forests became their bases and their homes. As their numbers grew, and as they worked alongside Polish partisan units, they made life increasingly difficult for the German occupiers. In May 1944, they took part in a major partisan battle, against German SS and Wehrmacht battalions and German Air Force units sent to destroy them. The account of that battle is one of the graphic high points of the memoir. So, too, is the sudden appearance of large numbers of German troops and tanks fleeing westward to avoid the advancing Red Army. For several hours, the danger was Russian artillery fire, as it pounded the retreating German forces. And then he saw a Russian colonel on horseback approaching through the meadow. "When he greeted us in Russian, I knew the worst was over. We had survived."

In 1985, as a result of an initiative in which Frank Blaichman had taken a leading part, a monument to the Jewish soldiers and partisans was unveiled at Yad Vashem in Jerusalem. George Schultz, the United States secretary of state, was the first American official to lay a wreath. In his own remarks at the ceremony, Frank Blaichman said, "I remember those comrades, the courageous, brave men and women who, together with us, answered the call of history: to defend Jewish lives, to defend Jewish honor and dignity. We are the fortunate ones; we are the survivors who must and will keep this legacy alive for generations to come."

Frank Blaichman's memoir does just that. It is a gripping story of suffering, endurance, and the triumph—against massive odds—of the human spirit, which will serve as a beacon of hope for all those who wonder how good can ever triumph over evil in a troubled world. Its lessons of courage and perseverance are as meaningful today as they ever were. Jews can hold their heads high when they read these pages; and all people, wherever they live, whatever struggles they face, can feel a sense of pride at what human beings can achieve when they take their destiny into their own hands.

Sir Martin Gilbert
London
February 23, 2009

The Wola, Bratnik, and Kozlowka Forest Areas

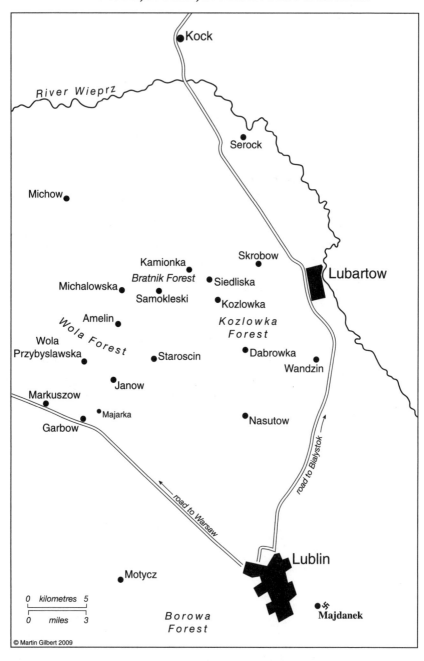

Kock

River Wieprz

Serock

Michow

Skrobow

Kamionka
Bratnik Forest
Michalowska
Samokleski
Siedliska
Kozlowka

Lubartow

Kozlowka
Forest

Amelin
Wola Forest
Wola
Przybyslawska
Staroscin
Dabrowka
Wandzin

Janow

Markuszow
Majarka
Nasutow

Garbow

road to Bialystok

road to Warsaw

Lublin

Motycz

Borowa
Forest

Majdanek

0 kilometres 5
0 miles 3

© Martin Gilbert 2009

RATHER DIE FIGHTING

CHAPTER I

DAYS OF TERROR AND A DECISION TO ESCAPE

ON THE MORNING OF SEPTEMBER I, 1939, the church bells of Kamionka rang as word spread that the mayor would be making an important announcement. We lived two hundred yards or so from the town hall, and my father and I hurried over to join the crowd that was gathering in the square. When the bells stopped ringing, the mayor came out to stand on the steps of the town hall, flanked by the chief of police and other officials. The Germans had invaded Poland, he said. They had crossed the border early that morning. We were at war. All reservists were to report to their units. The rest of us should stay calm and be vigilant. We were to report any strange comings and goings in the forests and on the roads leading into town. The mayor led us in singing the national anthem, and we also sang a song that said that the Polish people would never let the Germans spit in our faces. Then the crowd dispersed, and I went home with my father, who shared the news with my mother. I was sixteen.

Most members of our extended family lived in Kamionka, a town of about two thousand. There was no official ghetto — no walls — but our homes and our synagogue and our businesses were all in one section of town. We were a close-knit community of perhaps two hundred families. We had a synagogue, a house of study (a *beis medrash*), rabbis, tutors, a mohel, and a cantor. We also had a *mikvah*, a ritual bath, and when I was a little boy, my father would take me with him before *Shabbos* to the *mikvah* and to the *shvitz*, the steam bath. Sometimes gentile boys would call us names and throw stones at us, but by and large, the two groups — gentiles and Jews — got along well. Uncle Mayer, for instance, who dressed neatly in Hasidic garb and sported a little red beard, was a man to whom other men of his age tipped their hats.

Another member of the family who was widely respected was my paternal grandmother, my *bubbeh*, who ran a general store that served both Jews and gentiles, including farmers who came into the town to sell their produce on the market. Her name was Chana Gittel. She was a remarkable woman, my *bubbeh*. She collected money for the poor every Friday at noon, before sundown and Shabbat, in the marketplace. If a storyteller came to Kamionka for the Sabbath or a peddler needed lodgings for the night, he was referred to my *bubbeh*. She could be counted on to find them a bed, to give them money, to help in any way she could. Apart from running the store, she cultivated a vegetable garden behind her house. I remember that she grew scallions and pumpkins and strawberries, and garlic and tomatoes and radishes. Her husband, my paternal grand-father, was a Torah scholar who studied at home from dawn to dusk. It was my grandmother who, by making friends with those she dealt with, forged close bonds with farmers throughout the countryside that would prove crucial to my survival.

The mayor's announcement that the Germans had invaded Poland didn't mean much to me. We didn't talk about politics or foreign affairs at home. I had heard jokes about the German war machine, about how their tanks were made of plywood, and I had heard men boast that, if it came to war, a Pole wouldn't surrender even a single button from his uniform. Two of my father's brothers had emigrated to America in the 1920s, but this connection didn't result in any warnings from them that Father should get us out of the country before it was too late. We had no radio. Though we were on the main bus route that ran from Lublin, twelve miles to the south, to Warsaw, eighty miles to the northwest, I was completely ignorant of what was going on in the outside world.

There was little opportunity for advancement in our little shtetl. Young people tended to leave Kamionka as soon as they finished school. Many went off to Warsaw or some other big city to find work. That's what I had in mind to do. My father, who was a grain dealer, told me many times over that he did not want me to work in the grain business. He wanted me to concentrate on my schooling, to make something of myself. He himself was well respected, being a trusted middleman between the farmers in the area from whom he bought the grain and the merchants in Lublin and Lubartow to whom he sold it. He had the same compassionate nature as his mother. Unlike most other wholesalers in the region, he was willing to help farmers through the winter months when they needed to borrow money to support their families and buy seed for the spring planting. His name was Chaim Israel Blajchman. I called him Tateh. He was well over six feet tall, a good-looking man who practiced Orthodox Judaism.

My mother—Ita Lewin, whom I called Mameh—was an attractive woman, with beautiful long, black hair, very kind and capable. She came from a family of ultra-Orthodox Jews. Our family, though religiously observant, was more broad-minded than some of the other Orthodox families in town. My mother did not wear a wig or cover her hair during the week, although she always wore a hat when she went to synagogue. She was an excellent *balabusta,* a homemaker, a great cook, a wonderful mother to her seven children—three sons and four daughters.

We lived simply but comfortably in a four-room apartment in a stucco house on the north side of the main road from Lublin to Lubartow. It was close to the marketplace and close to the bus station. It was also directly across the street from the police station, a location that proved useful when the Germans occupied the town. My parents had their own bedroom. I shared a room with my brothers, Leibel and Shmuel. Sara, who was two years older than I, shared a room with her younger sisters, Esther and Faiga and Sheindel, who was just a toddler. There were two stoves—the brick stove in the kitchen, for cooking; and the gas-iron stove, which we used to warm up our dining room and living room in the winter months.

During the summer, Kamionka became a kind of resort town, not for the rich, but for middle-class people from Warsaw and Lublin who wanted to enjoy a week in the country. Just outside of town, there were broad meadows with a brook running through them, where horses grazed and ran free, and where I played as a boy. Beyond the meadows, about two miles to the south, there was Bratnik Forest, part of the much larger Kozlowka Forest, which was owned by Count Zamoyski, one of the great noblemen of Poland. We often spent Sunday afternoon picnicking in Bratnik Forest. Blueberries grew in the woods and I often used to go there to pick blueberries with my friends, and sometimes in the fall I would go along with the women who gathered mushrooms, so I got to know which ones were edible.

The area was dotted with small castles nowhere near as grand as the Zamoyski residence, but handsome and with beautiful grounds. I especially remember Baron Kuszel's castle in Samoklesk. My father did business with the baron and took me along with him once. Peacocks were parading and several puppies were romping around while their mother lay in the shade, watching over them. Suddenly, one of the peacocks went after one of the puppies, and the mother dog, thinking I was the one who had attacked her puppy, ran up and gripped my hand. When I think of that castle, that's what comes to mind—being attacked by that dog.

Castles and their parks were part of the landscape, which, where it wasn't forested, was largely given over to grain fields. The rich farmers, who owned large plots of land, lived in solid houses with tin roofs and had huge barns in which to store their hay and stall their livestock in winter. The poor farmers lived in log houses with thatched roofs and earthen floors and scratched out a meager living on their small plots of land. They were truly dirt poor. The main crops were wheat, rye, barley, and oats. The whole economy was based on the grain trade and timber, with Lublin and Lubartow serving as depots and rail centers from which these commodities were transported throughout Poland and beyond.

This was the rural world in which I grew up, in which horses drew wagons, people read by candlelight, and teenage boys made ice skates out of old sickles and took girls on sleigh rides in winter. The announcement of the outbreak of war didn't change anything in our lives. The war was a long way away. It didn't come to Kamionka until suddenly, in mid-September, Jews fleeing from Warsaw and western Poland started streaming into town, hoping to cross the Bug River into Russian-occupied territory, eighty miles to the east. They thought life would be better under the Russians, whose troops had moved into eastern Poland on September 17, than under the Germans.

They came on foot, on bicycle, by horse and wagon, and by car. I remember one car in particular: a Czech-made, navy-blue convertible Tatra. It was packed with suitcases and well-dressed city people. The car had run out of gas. The people were in a panic. They didn't know what to do. Finally, after frantically searching for a can of gas, they decided to abandon the car, buy a few bicycles, and hire a team of horses and a wagon to get them and their baggage out of town. They left the Tatra behind in the town square.

The procession of refugees kept coming, with families carrying as much as they could load onto a horse-drawn wagon or pull on a handcart. Many of our people joined the stream of refugees. One of them was my cousin Shmuel Blajchman.

Then the day came when it wasn't just Jews, but Polish soldiers, hundreds of them, in full retreat, throwing away their rifles, trying to trade their uniforms for civilian clothes. One officer showed up at our door. When my father let him in, the officer collapsed on a bed. The man had been walking for days. It was a time of terror. One day I biked over to Lubartow on an errand and heard bombs exploding close to the train station. When I got home and told my parents about the bombardment, my father was terribly upset. I shouldn't be riding around on my bike. I should stay close to home. He had served in the Polish Army in the First World War and knew what war was like.

By the end of September, the fighting was all over. In early October, the first German soldiers appeared in Kamionka and the first anti-Jewish decrees were posted on public buildings. Then a regiment of Germans arrived with artillery pieces and set up camp in the meadows outside of town. A few days passed without incident. Then the soldiers rounded up a group of Hasidim, gave them shovels, and ordered them to dig ditches. As the Hasidim dug, the soldiers beat them with their rifle butts and made fun of them, cursing them, laughing at them when they fell. When the Hasidim finished digging the ditches, the soldiers made them fill them in again and went on beating them. I watched from a distance, shaken, and fantasized about taking revenge.

The German authorities ordered the Jewish community to establish a Jewish council, or Judenrat. The Germans would tell the Judenrat what to do, what restrictions to impose, which Jews to arrest, which to send to work, and so on. If the Judenrat didn't do what the Germans ordered them to do, they would be imprisoned or shot. Kiveleh the shoemaker and five others whose names I don't recall became members of the Judenrat. Fiszel Wacholder signed up with the Judenrat police, which enforced the orders issued by the Judenrat, which was carrying out the Germans' orders. It was a forge-linked chain of collaboration, with the Germans getting the Jews to do the dirty work for them.

The Germans then began to conscript young Jewish men to work as slave laborers in the estates around Kamionka. They were needed to replace Polish farmworkers who had been drafted into the Polish Army and had been either killed or taken prisoner, or had escaped across the border to the Russian side. If the Judenrat failed to deliver enough workers, the Germans would stage a roundup.

At first, the labor was fieldwork—bringing in the harvest. Then the brook had to be widened and ditches dug to drain the wetlands. The men had to work two days a week. Their wages were a week's supply of bread, cheese, marmalade, and margarine; the package could be sold on the black market for fifty or sixty zlotys. I hated the fieldwork and asked Mendel, a former classmate, if he would take my shift if I paid him. He said he would if I paid him two zlotys a day. My father was willing to pay the two zlotys. I never worked in the fields again. But I was on hand when the Germans gave out the monthly food package, which I always gave to Mameh. That helped us get through the lean times.

Toward the end of that year—in December, as I recall—we were ordered to wear white armbands with the Star of David. All Jews were also ordered to file detailed reports of their financial assets and were forbidden to have more than two thousand zlotys, or about two hundred dollars, in the house at any time. All Jewish businesses were confiscated and given to gentiles, and so from one day to the next, my father, like many others, had no means of income, except for the occasional odd job at Baron Kuszel's estate. Jewish artists and artisans were no longer permitted to practice their craft or trade. Jewish teachers could no longer teach, and Jewish doctors could no longer treat non-Jews. Then the Nazis rounded up all those they regarded as people who might organize some form of resistance—intellectuals, teachers, artists, and rabbis. Uncle Mayer, the Hasid with the little red beard, was one of them. They were taken away to Majdanek Concentration Camp, in Lublin. I never saw my uncle again.

At this time, too, all Jews were forced to move out of their homes and into apartments in a poor section of town. We moved into a four-room apartment above a bakery owned by a gentile couple, Stephan and Wanda Dudek. Our large family was now crowded into a very small space. My sister Sara moved in with us for a time. She had been working at a fabric store in Lubartow owned by Jews, and had lost her job when the shop was liquidated. After staying with us for a while, she went to Kotzk to look after our aunt Frymet's children. I never saw Sara again.

After the Germans had carried out many roundups, which were always unannounced and sent a wave of terror through the community, with no one knowing who would be taken next, I vowed that I would not let myself be taken. I began asking people what they were planning to do. Most of them said they would abide by God's will or things like that. That was the Orthodox way. The Germans had commandeered our shul for their office. Secret synagogues sprang up in houses here and there. We built a sukkah in the back of our house, but there were no festivities. Simchas Torah went by without dancing in the streets. For Pesach, we baked our matzohs and held our seders in secret.

Resistance seemed impossible. We had heard what the Nazis did if a German was killed: they would round up as many as a hundred Jews and kill them in retaliation. That's what they had done in Warsaw and many other cities. So even if we had possessed weapons, we wouldn't have been able to use them for fear of what would happen to our fellow Jews.

Food rationing had been imposed on Kamionka. I had my bike. I started bringing food into town. It was Stephan

Dudek who helped me with my trading. He telephoned relatives throughout the area and asked if they needed anything I could bring from the country, and if they could provide the things I needed in exchange. He let me hide my bike in the shed beside his house, which was on the outskirts of town. I kept my dealings a closely guarded secret; only my family and the Dudeks knew what I was doing. Although I could have been shot for not wearing the Star of David armband, I left it at home when I rode out of town. Without the armband, I could pass as a gentile because I spoke Polish fluently and without an accent. This gave me freedom to move around. I attached a basket to the handlebars of my bike and a basket behind the seat and started biking to nearby villages and to the homes of farmers who had done business with my father or my grandmother. The Germans hadn't gotten around to confiscating my grandmother's store. I don't know why. Perhaps because the shop was small.

My grandmother provided me with items from her store; tobacco, saccharine, and yarn were the most popular. I traded them for butter, cheese, eggs, poultry. In the process, I came to know the farmers she dealt with, the ones she trusted, the ones who were willing to deal with Jews, even when it was illegal to do so. Week by week, my route expanded. I put on heavier tires and inner tubes. Eventually, I bicycled as far as Lubartow and Lublin. Then one day, I loaded my bike with about a hundred pounds of meat and set off for Warsaw. I joined a group of bikers in order to make myself as inconspicuous as possible. We rode in the deep drainage ditches along the side of the roads.

I kept to the middle of the group. I rested when they rested and ate when they ate.

We were taking a break on the side of the road when a squad of Ukrainians in black uniforms beat and robbed a Hasidic family riding on a horse-drawn wagon. These Ukrainians worked alongside the Germans and were just as vicious. When they were done with the family, they came over to talk to us. They said we had nothing to worry about: they only beat up Jews. I decided that the Warsaw run was too risky, and, though I completed my run, I never went to Warsaw again.

One time when I was biking to Lublin, keeping to back roads as usual, I saw two German gendarmes coming my way. I saw them before they saw me and turned off onto a narrow lane that angled back to the main road. I hadn't gone far before I ran into another detachment of gendarmes. I was scared but kept on biking, and they didn't stop me. They must have thought the other gendarmes had already checked me out. Again, I had been lucky, but I decided not to take that route again.

Nineteen forty-one was a year of increasing hardship. The Nazi propaganda machine encouraged our neighbors to despise us and hate us. We could be beaten on any pretext. If we saluted a German, he might decide to beat us because we were not human enough to salute a German. If we failed to salute him, we could be beaten for being disrespectful. German gendarmes began appearing without notice to search people's apartments for contraband. One day, they searched my uncle Moishe's house and found the meat he had prepared, in secret, for *Shabbos*. The gendarmes led Uncle Moishe out to the Catholic cemetery and shot him. Uncle Moishe had been a cattle dealer. Father was very close to Moishe, his older brother. They played cards at each other's house every Saturday night when the *Shabbos* was over. The Germans ordered some Poles to bury Uncle Moishe somewhere behind the cemetery. None of us were allowed to attend the burial. Killings had become an almost daily occurrence. Now it was one of our own. My uncle's family suspected that a Jewish boarder in their home had gossiped about the forbidden meat and somehow the Germans had heard.

A few weeks later, my cousin Brucha was killed — shot in her bed — after the Germans found fresh bread in my grandmother's house. Why they didn't kill my grandmother at the same time, I don't know.

That fall, I tried to find out what had happened to my uncle Mayer Lewin. Stephan Dudek had a brother named Kazimeirz who lived in Lublin. I would occasionally spend the night at the Dudeks' after bringing supplies in from the country. Our two families had developed a close relationship, and the Dudeks treated me as if I was a member of their family. One night when I was staying with them, I told them we were worried about my uncle because we hadn't heard from him since he was taken. A few weeks later, Stephan said he had heard that Poles who were building barracks in Majdanek-Tatarski, across the highway from Majdanek proper, often socialized with the German guards, and these Poles had contact with guards who, for a price, could get a prisoner out of the concentration camp. When I heard this, I told my father, and he said that we should try to find out if Uncle Mayer was still alive, and if he was, we should see if we could buy him out of the camp. On one of my trips to Lublin, I asked Kazimeirz if he knew of someone I could talk to about this. He said he would try to find a contact. One person he got in touch with didn't want to get involved. But Kazimeirz didn't give up. A few days later, he found a man who provided me with a guide who would lead me to a kind of roadhouse where I was to meet a man named Walter, who could make contact with a guard. My guide led me through side streets and fields and pointed to a building with a red roof. He described Walter's appearance and said he would be waiting for me. I was scared stiff, but I went into the roadhouse and saw the man, and we sat and talked for about ten minutes. We didn't talk about getting Uncle Mayer out of the camp for fear that our conversation might be overheard. I had brought a letter telling Walter what we wanted: proof that Uncle Mayer was still alive.

"If you find that he's alive," I said, "we can negotiate."

Walter seemed ready to do business, but said it would take him a couple of days. Then he left. When he left, I panicked. The camp was only a few hundred yards away. I might be caught and taken away. I realized that it had been a mistake to deliver the letter myself. I could have made some other arrangement. I was so nervous that I had to go to the bathroom. A man came in and stood right next to me. He saw that I was circumcised and said, "You're a Jew." Then he ran out into the restaurant and I ran out the back way and got on my bicycle and bicycled away as fast as I could. I hid in a field of rye and tried to calm down. I never came back to Majdanek. It was too risky.

As the year wore on, our gentile neighbors, who could travel freely, began to share with us terrifying information that they had picked up from train conductors and Ukrainians who worked in the camps. People who lived around Majdanek were complaining that "the air smelled as if they are burning cats," making a terrible joke of the mass murder of humans. My father and others realized that what was happening to others could happen to us—that we would be taken to one or another of the death camps in our region: Treblinka, Sobibor, and Majdanek.

In May 1942, there was a deportation from the nearby town of Markuszow. Hundreds of Jews, tipped off by the Judenrat that they were going to be sent to death camps, fled into the forest at Wola Przybyslawska. Many of them escaped to Kamionka. Twenty of them were recaptured when Polish informers tipped off the Nazis, who ordered the local Judenrat to round them up. The Judenrat sent out its Jewish police to conduct a house-to-house search.

The search began at about eleven in the morning. My father and I were visiting my uncle Moishe's grieving family when one of the fugitives burst through the door. Seeing the terror in the man's face, my father shoved him into another room and shut the door. A moment later, the Judenrat policeman started pounding on the front door. My father didn't open it until he had told the fugitive to escape through a window. When he finally opened the door, he struck the policeman so hard that the man fell to the floor. Then my father screamed at him, "How could you chase your own brothers and hand them over to the enemy?" The policeman did not answer. He just got up and went off to knock on the door of the next house.

All the men and women who were rounded up that day were taken to the meadow where I used to play as a boy and shot.

One of those who escaped from Markuszow to Kamionka was Blimka Rubinstein, a beautiful, brown-haired, blue-eyed girl. When I met her later, she told me that, after being captured by the Judenrat police, she and the other Markuszow escapees had been handed over to the Polish police and the Germans. While they were standing in front of the police station, one of the Jewish informers who had tipped off the Germans walked up to her and said in Polish, "You are a Czech. Don't say a word." He pulled her out of the lineup and led her to a spot where she could slip away. I imagine that the informer, Moishe Klerer, did not have the heart to send such a beautiful young girl to what he knew would be certain death.

At one of the last bar mitzvahs we attended, I asked each of the elders the same question: "Why do they want to kill us?"

They all gave me the same answer: "The only crime we have committed was that we were born Jews."

I said, "Why don't we do something about it?"

And the answer was always the same: "With God's help, we will overcome all the difficulties. If God wills it otherwise, we have no choice but to go along."

Every once in a while, without any warning, another group of Jews was rounded up and deported. We feared it was only a matter of time before the Germans came for us. I was used to moving around on my own on my bicycle. I loved the freedom it gave me. I knew my way around the back-country lanes, and I was born with an unerring sense of direction. Also, I felt sure I could pass as a gentile. I decided that I had to escape. I didn't know how, but I knew I couldn't just wait to be picked up and killed. Better to get shot trying to get away than stay and die.

CHAPTER 11

FROM FARMHOUSE TO FOREST

IN AUGUST 1942, my neighbor Jankel, Sura Dina's son—that's what people called him in town; I never knew what his surname was—approached me. Jankel was a refugee from Warsaw who was living with Kamionka cousins. We weren't close friends, so I was surprised when he asked what I planned to do if we found out that we were going to be deported. I said I had no specific plan, but that I had made up my mind that I was not going to be deported and shut up in some ghetto or camp. He gave me a searching look and then asked if he could join me wherever I went. I felt flattered that this man who was twelve years older and had served in the Polish Army wanted to join up with me.

"Two are better than one," I said.

Later, he told me that he had approached me because he knew that I had friends among the farmers in the countryside; he thought that some of them might have offered to hide me. He was right.

One day shortly after this, a passenger car with German officers, followed by two trucks carrying German soldiers, pulled up in front of the police station. I figured that they were planning to carry out another roundup. I slipped out of the house and ran out of town and into a field where the rye was almost ready to be harvested, and I hid there. Other Jews came running out to hide in the field. Everything was quiet for a while. Then the Germans started shouting, *"Aufstehen. Komm' hier."* (Stand up. Come here.) Some of the people stood up. I heard dogs barking and was afraid that they would find me. But I lay low, and the Germans and the dogs and the Jews who had given themselves up went away.

I stayed there for about an hour, crouched and listening and wondering how I would ever get back home. When I stood up, I saw a haystack under a thatched roof a couple of hundred feet away, and I crawled toward it. The haystack was about twenty feet high and twenty feet thick. I put on my hat and, after looking all around to see if anyone was watching, climbed to the top. I found I wasn't alone. A Jewish man in his fifties was lying there. I told him to dig himself in, but for some reason he just lay there.

"If you get caught," I said, "don't tell anyone that I'm here."

I dug myself down into the stack until I was near the bottom. I poked little holes in the stack to get air.

Half an hour later, I heard men speaking Polish. They saw the man and brought him down. They didn't ask him any questions, but they jabbed pitchforks into the stack from all sides. I was just out of range. They took him away. I lay there until nightfall, then crawled out from the bottom and ran home. On the way, I learned from my neighbors that a lot of young Jews had been rounded up, presumably for slave labor. When I entered our apartment, my parents almost sobbed with relief. I had been away so long they were sure that I had been caught.

In early September, the Germans announced that they were going to create a big ghetto in Lubartow for all the Jews in the region. We were just being resettled, they said. Then, on October 8, in the afternoon, word spread that all the Jews of Kamionka were to be deported to Lubartow the next morning. Jankel met me in the town square. We decided to slip out of town that night.

When I returned to our apartment, no one spoke. My parents sat frozen, knowing full well what deportation meant. I am sure they understood that I was not going to go with them. I also knew that neither my parents nor my brothers and sisters would come with me. They were too young. My only hope was that they would all be taken to a ghetto, where life might be hard, but not to a camp, where they would be worked to death or killed. I looked at my parents' faces and, though I feared we would never see each other again, I could not embrace them. The children would know this meant goodbye. We were all holding ourselves in, trying to get through this day of waiting. All I could say was, *"Zeits gezunt."* (Be healthy.) "Maybe I'll see you in Lubartow."

When night fell, I walked out of the apartment and down the stairs and into the street. Bread was all I took in the way of provisions. Jankel was waiting for me around the corner. We took side streets and cut through backyards. He asked me where we were going and I said that I would probably go first to the Klos family, with whom my grandmother and I had done business. They had told me I could hide out on their farm if need be. The farm was in the village of Kierzkowka.

On the way, we stopped at Count Zamoyski's palace in Kozlowka, where two Jewish boys I knew, Leibel and Nisson, worked as slave laborers in the kitchen. We wanted to warn them of the deportation and ask if we could spend the night there. It turned out they had already heard about the deportation. They asked the kitchen manager if we could spend the night in a spare room off the kitchen. She said we could and made us sandwiches and showed us the room. But we couldn't sleep. We talked all night about what was happening to our families and our friends. Leibel and Nisson decided to join us.

We slipped out at about five in the morning. We walked in the woods parallel to the main road, then hid in a wooded area about a hundred yards from the road. We wanted to watch the trucks go by on their way to Lubartow. We wanted to witness the deportation, and maybe get a glimpse of our relatives.

At about nine, we heard whispering. We crept off to see where it was coming from and discovered a group of about thirty Jews who had also run from Kamionka. Two of them were Judenrat policemen. They had come to witness the deportation too.

We sat for maybe two hours, waiting for the trucks to pass. Finally, some of the older men sent two boys, who were blond and blue-eyed and could pass as gentiles, to find out what was going on. They were back in ten minutes. They had asked a farmer if he knew what had happened in Kamionka. He said he had heard that German gendarmes and Polish police had driven all the Jews out of their houses. Those who couldn't run fast enough were shot on the spot. The rest had been taken to Lubartow. It was strange: we had all come to this place to watch the trucks go by, and we hadn't seen or heard a single truck.

We sat in a circle and started to debate what to do. Some of the men said we should find a deeper forest to hide in. Others said that without food or weapons, we could never survive in the forest. Or not for long. Others said we should hide with families in villages. But someone pointed out that there were a lot of Jew-hating Poles who would be glad to kill us or turn us in to the Nazis. The two Judenrat policemen tried to talk us into going to Lubartow. Our chances of survival in the ghetto would be much better than in the forest or with farmers, they said. The Germans would need Judenrat police to keep order in the ghetto. We young men could apply for the jobs.

The talk went on, everyone having his say. I kept quiet until one of the men turned to me and said, "You've been sitting here saying nothing. What are *you* planning to do?"

I told them that some farmers had promised to hide me, and that Jankel and I planned to try our luck with them. The older men said that this was a stupid idea: the farmers would beat us to death and bury our bodies in unmarked graves. The Judenrat policemen urged us, again, to continue on our way to Lubartow to see if we could find jobs with the Judenrat police in the new ghetto. Finally, the others agreed that this might be our best hope. And Jankel agreed, and got up and started walking toward Lubartow. I got up and started walking too.

I had walked maybe a hundred yards when I saw something rising up on the horizon that stopped me. It was the cross on top of the big church in Lubartow. It was a moment in my life I will never forget and never be able to explain. An inner voice spoke to me: "You promised you would not go freely into any ghetto, and now that's what you are setting out to do."

I could not go farther. I was not going to go with these others. I hoped that Jankel would come with me, and I asked him to, but he said no. He had made up his mind. He was going with the others. So I said, as I had said to my parents when I left them, *"Zeits gezunt,"* and started to walk away. But now Usher, the butcher's son, and a Jew from Warsaw, whose name I've forgotten, had second thoughts, and they started to follow me. Usher asked what I was planning to do. I said I planned to stay in the area, hiding out here and there until I could figure out what to do next. He didn't like the idea. He turned and ran to catch up with the others. The Warsaw Jew continued with me.

I started walking through the fields in the general direction of the Klos farm, disappointed with Jankel, who had promised to come with me. The Warsaw Jew began to talk to me. He said some Jewish families from Markuszow were hiding in a forest near Wola Przybyslawska. He described the underground bunkers they had made and urged me to go there with him and see if there was a place we could hide. I told him about my farmer friend, Alexsander Klos, who had promised to help me. The Warsaw Jew tried to talk me into going with him and I tried to talk him into coming with me. When a farmer offered us a lift in his wagon, we jumped on and went on trying to talk each other around. Finally, unable to persuade the Warsaw Jew to come with me, I jumped off the wagon. I never saw him again.

I watched the wagon disappear down the lane. I had never felt so alone in my life. I felt overwhelmed and terrified. My mind was racing. Had I done the right thing in leaving my family and going off by myself? I felt guilty, as if I had abandoned them. But what could I have done for them? And how much longer could I hope to live? Maybe the older men were right: the Jew haters would be sure to find me. If they didn't kill me, the winter would. It had started to rain, and I started to cry and I couldn't stop. I pulled myself together. There was one consolation: I was still free.

When I reached the Klos farm, Alexsander and his wife, Alfreda, greeted me like a long-lost son. When they saw the state I was in, they did their best to comfort me. They assured me that the war would be over as soon as the Russian Army advanced. The two Klos children chatted with me as they usually did when I came by on my bike, while Mrs. Klos prepared a meal for me. As I ate, I couldn't help but think of the risk that the Kloses were taking by sheltering me. If the

Germans found out, they would burn the house and kill the whole family. After supper, seeing how tired I was, Mrs. Klos urged me to go to bed. I said I would rather sleep in the barn than in the house; that way, if anyone found me, the Kloses could claim they had no idea who I was. They agreed.

Mrs. Klos brought pillows and blankets and sheets out to the barn, and she and Alexsander stayed with me for at least an hour, trying to calm me down and reassure me. The barn was huge—more than twenty thousand square feet—but the next morning, when Mrs. Klos came in to see how I had slept, she found me lying on the far side of the barn. Apparently, I had been so restless that I had rolled the whole width of the barn. She brought me breakfast—cheese, bread, butter, and milk.

I couldn't eat a bite. I was too upset, worried about my family. I drank the milk and hid the rest of the food in the hay because I didn't want Mrs. Klos to think I hadn't eaten the breakfast she had prepared for me. At noon, both Mr. and Mrs. Klos came out to the barn.

Mr. Klos said he had both good news and bad. I asked him to give me the bad news first. He told me that all the Jews who had been deported to Lubartow had been taken to the train station and sent off to an unknown destination. When I heard this, I wished for my own death. I knew I would never see my family again.

Then he said, "The good news is that I have in-laws in the villages around here. I told them about you. They gave me their word that they would treat you the same way we do, like a member of the family."

I thanked the Kloses. I told them I could never repay them for their kindness. After we had talked for a time, they went off to do their chores, and later Mrs. Klos brought me lunch, but, again, I couldn't eat. I sat looking through the cracks in the wall. When it was dark, I stole out of the barn and made my way into Kamionka to see Wanda Dudek. I wanted to hear from her what had happened.

She was a widow now; Stephan had died of diabetes. She hugged and kissed me and invited me to stay with her. Then she described, in almost exactly the same words Alexsander Klos had used, what had happened to the Jews of Kamionka—how they had been deported to Lubartow and not put in a ghetto but loaded onto a train and taken off to an unknown destination. I could no longer have any hope that my family would be spared. I burst into tears. It was all too painful, the thought of my family being taken away by the Germans, who knew no pity.

When I could speak again, I thanked Wanda for her offer to shelter me but told her it would be dangerous, for her and for me. The houses in Kamionka were close to one another; someone would be sure to notice my presence. I said goodbye and left.

Out on the street, I was surprised to see little Mottele Reis, who was only ten years old, walking all by himself.

"What are you doing here?" I said.

He said he had come back to pick up some things his family had left behind. I asked him where his family was. He said that they were in Bratnik Forest and that many other Jews were there too, hiding in underground bunkers. I asked him to tell me exactly where they were — on which side of the road. I was eager to talk to them. Maybe they could give me more information about the deportation; maybe someone had seen my family. Mottele told me that I would find them "about half a mile into the forest, to the right."

By the time I got back to the farm, the Kloses had gone to bed. The next morning, I told them that I would be gone for a couple of days. They didn't ask any questions but gave me their blessing, and Mrs. Klos made me some sandwiches and gave me blankets.

I set out on the path, thinking of my family. It was a Sunday. The sky was overcast; it was turning cold. I had rolled up the two blankets and tied them to a stick, together with the sandwiches that Mrs. Klos had given me, which I slung over my shoulder. I was wearing a sweater but no overcoat. I hadn't thought that I might be spending the winter in a forest. I hadn't been able to think that far ahead. I made my way through the fields, heading southwest, toward Bratnik Forest, hoping to find the campsite that Mottele had described.

Bratnik Forest was an old-growth forest, mostly pine, about five miles long and two miles wide, intersected by lanes used by farmers and villagers. Mottele had given me good directions. I had no trouble finding the campsite. No one challenged me. No lookouts had been posted. Through the trees I could make out a group of about fifteen people, many of whom I knew from Kamionka. Mottele Reis's family was there, and the Klerers, and the Lambergs. The Reises had been in the leather business, the Klerers in the horse-trading business, and the Lambergs had owned Kamionka's confectionery, which also served as the bus depot. They all greeted me warmly. There were many other people whom I recognized. There must have been a hundred people at this campsite, and spending these last three days in the forest had taken its toll. They looked weary and dejected, without hope.

Scattered around the campsite were about a dozen well-camouflaged underground bunkers. Each bunker had been dug near a tree, making it easier for the people who slept there to locate their bunker. The door was a plank on which leaves and branches had been glued. The entrance holes were so narrow you had to crawl in on all fours. You couldn't stand up inside. The bunkers were about eight feet wide and twenty feet long, with logs reinforcing the dirt walls. Thick posts in each corner and one in the center provided support. A tinsmith had installed vents to let in fresh air.

When I crawled inside the bunker I had been assigned to and tried to get to sleep, I felt that I had buried myself, that I was in a grave. I hadn't wanted to be trapped in a ghetto. Now I felt trapped in this underground chamber. I couldn't sleep. When I heard deer running, my first thought was, It's the Germans. When the wind stirred the branches, I was sure Germans were stealing up on us.

The people had brought as much food as they could carry, together with the tools they needed to build these bunkers. They had brought potatoes, red beets, barrels of sauerkraut, onions, garlic, salt, pepper, and sugar, and lots of jars of goose fat—all the ingredients needed to make thick soups. Most of the food was stored in holes dug deep enough into the ground to keep it cool. People had also brought huge loaves of bread that could keep for as long as two months without going stale. It was clear that they had made careful preparations for their escape. Neighbors had been in on the planning and preparations for days, and nobody had let us in on the secret.

On my second day at the campsite, I felt that I wasn't as welcome as I had thought I was. Jankel Klerer, whom I knew only through seeing him on High Holidays when he came back from Warsaw to be with his family, and Avram Reis started to question me. Avram wanted to know where I had spent the past couple of days. I told him that I had spent the first night in the kitchen at the castle and the second night at the Kloses'. Then he wanted to know how I had found my way to the forest, and I explained that I knew the area very well from trading with farmers throughout the countryside and that, to avoid being seen, I had kept to small lanes and roads that cut through the forest. I knew my way around.

Then Avram and Jankel and I sat on a log, and it was Jankel's turn to question me. He wanted to know how I had found out about their hideout—who had told me? I told him about meeting his nephew Mottele the night I had slipped away from the Kloses' farm, and how he had given me very clear directions. Then I turned to Avram and told him he could ask Mottele, who was right there at the campsite, if he didn't believe me. That settled that, but they weren't done with me yet. They wanted to know how I had managed to bicycle around the countryside for more than two years without a permit. I explained that I had removed my armband when I biked out of town, and that I was willing to take risks to help my family and that I felt fairly safe because I spoke Polish without an accent and that I found that I had an uncanny sense of direction, so I wasn't afraid of getting lost. The three of us talked for nearly an hour. When they were done with their questions and I had told them my whole story, we all got up and they patted me on the back, saying that they admired my courage. I felt I had won their confidence and gained their respect.

That night, I found it hard to get to sleep. I kept thinking about the interview. My first thought was, Why had they been so suspicious of me? Then I began to feel that it was a good thing they had forced me to say so much that I would otherwise never have told anyone. My willingness to take risks might have seemed like boasting. Finally, I felt lucky that I had met these people whose way of thinking—not to go freely to the slaughter—I shared. My talk with the two older men opened me up, and after this I felt able to voice my opinion about many issues.

I began to speak out very freely. I wasn't afraid of what people might say because if they didn't like me, I could always go back to the Kloses. The others had nowhere to go. At the same time, I was more vigilant than others, always concerned about our safety. I felt that my chances of survival were better if I was with a group, so my survival depended on theirs.

I had been surprised by the lack of lookouts when I first

arrived. Now, when I saw how the meals were being prepared, with the cooking being done over an open fire that sent up columns of smoke, I was alarmed, but I was new and young and thought that this was just how things were done out here. A day or two later, it occurred to me that it was the green wood that made the fires so smoky. I asked for some rope and went out into the forest and came back with two bundles of dry wood. I found the dry wood under the thick cover of fallen leaves by poking around with a stick. It wasn't just lying around, waiting to be picked up. The dry-wood fire still smoked, but a lot less than the green. Then it occurred to me that we could keep the smoke down if we hung blankets on ropes stretched a feet few above the fire. That helped. From then on, our fires were virtually smokeless. Where these ideas came from, I don't know. They just seemed like common sense to me.

There were times when I thought of going back to the Klos family, but people at the campsite said that, as soon as the deportations began, even formerly friendly neighbors had started turning in hidden Jews. They felt that they had to behave like their most vicious neighbors. They turned into killers who could claim that they were only obeying the law. It was safer to be vicious than to show mercy. By now, the Kloses might have realized that sheltering a Jew had gotten more dangerous than before. They might let me stay for a day or two and then ask me to leave, for the sake of their children. Where would I go? They had said that other farmers would take me in. Now I wasn't sure I could trust people I didn't know. So I decided to remain at the campsite, at least for the time being.

We had to get more supplies. A group of women went out to see if they could buy produce from friendly farmers. They returned in tears. They had kept to small country lanes and had tried to escape notice by wearing head scarves like those worn by Polish peasant women, but hoodlums had seen them and chased them down. Several of the women had been beaten and robbed. Some had been raped. Nobody had expected that this could happen. It was a frightening development. We had to bring food into the camp somehow or other. I talked to Jankel Klerer and Avram Reis. I said we had to find some way of protecting our women. They agreed. But how? What means of defense did we have? None.

About a week after this first incident, another group of women who went out to get milk and other staples came back saying that they had been beaten and driven out of several small villages. I asked them what sort of weapons the hoodlums carried. "Sticks and knives," they said.

That's when I came up with the idea of forming a defense unit to be used not in the villages, where we would always be outnumbered, but in case the hoodlums followed our women back to the campsite. In late October, we formed a group of twelve, all of us roughly the same age. About twenty other young men and boys said that they might join but wanted to wait and see how things went. We chose Jankel Klerer as our commander. He was thirty years old, six feet tall, and had served in the Polish Army, and we all had come to respect his judgment. Max and Simcha, two other members of our group, had also served in the army; they had been taken prisoner and had escaped from the POW camp in Lublin. Another member was Avram Reis, little Mottele's uncle. Then there was my cousin Froim, who had escaped from the carriage-wheel factory in Warsaw and had brought his little brother, Usher, with him. And there was Shabse, who had sold newspapers in Warsaw. He was about six feet tall, very solidly built—a good soul, but not very bright. The same could be said of Moishe Sznader, except that he was shorter. Moishe Leib, a shoemaker from Markuszow, was as tall as Shabse, but very thin.

Others in our unit were Hershzel and Yosel Herszman, both from Staroscin, a village close to Kamionka. Yosel was a grain dealer. Hershzel was a tailor, a moody man who brooded about his wife and children. He said he "knew" that they were all dead. Josef Hershman was the son of a grain dealer, and he, too, was from Staroscin. Then there was Mendel Lamberg, whose family had been taken to Lubartow in the same deportation as mine. He was a cousin of the Mendel who had taken my shift as a slave laborer. He was about three years older than I—a tailor by trade, a bit of a dreamer.

They called me *Suchy Franek* (Skinny Frank). Though I was among the youngest in our unit, Jankel Klerer and others sought my advice on the best way to move through the forest to get to a certain village or farmhouse without attracting attention. I knew the terrain, and I knew many of the people.

I think many in the camp thought that they were safe now that they were living in the forest. They thought that, since the Poles had taken everything away from them — their businesses, their houses, their possessions — they would let them alone, as long as they kept out of sight. Others were more realistic. They thought our chances of survival were slim. We would either starve or freeze to death or be hunted down. If the hunters found us, we would be killed because we had nothing with which to defend ourselves.

Jankel Klerer found ways of keeping up our morale. He put us through a training course in which we used sticks for rifles. He taught us how to fall without "shooting" ourselves, and how to crawl on our elbows and knees while we moved our "rifles" forward. He taught us how to walk silently in the woods — to avoid stepping on dry branches, to whisper instead of talking out loud. He emphasized the importance of always being on the alert for suspicious sounds or signs of the presence of others. And after our women suffered abuse at the hands of the hoodlums, he posted guards around the campsite and scouts along the edge of the forest to warn the rest of us in case the hoodlums followed the women into the forest.

One day Jankel took twelve of us men out to buy supplies in Michalowska Kolony. (The countryside was full of "Kolonys" — small settlements of maybe a dozen or two houses.) We divided into three groups. My group approached the first house. When I showed the woman our money, she slammed the door and started screaming out the window, "Jews! Jews!" Suddenly, all the women in the village were banging pots and pans, making a terrific racket. The woman at the first house had sounded the alarm. Men came running from all directions while the women went on screaming, "Jews! Jews!" The men were all carrying pitchforks. We ran for our lives.

Once we reached the edge of the forest, we sat down, caught our breath, thought things over, and decided to see if we might have better luck at isolated farmhouses. And we did. We went up to the door and offered the farmers money and they sold us their produce, and we returned to the campsite with a good load of supplies. But the village experience had shocked us. We had never realized how fiercely these village people hated us. We had no doubt that, if they had caught up with us, those men would have stuck their pitchforks into us, maybe even killed us. Providing food for a group as large as ours was going to be very difficult, and would only get worse when the snow fell and we could be easily tracked back to our campsite.

We now rationed what was left of our provisions. To boost our confidence when we went out in search of food, we stole pitchforks from neighboring farms and had a friendly black-smith remove all the tines except the middle one, which he shortened and straightened. Then we attached shoulder straps to the handle. From a distance and at dusk, our single-tine pitchforks could be taken for rifles.

The first time I went out to buy food, I took two men with me, all three of us equipped with our pitchfork rifles. We went to one of Bubbeh's customers, a farmer named Meksola— someone I could trust. I left my rifle with the men and went up to the door. When I knocked, Mr. Meksola opened the door and invited me in.

"Mr. Meksola," I said, "we need help. I came by back ways to avoid being seen, so it wouldn't be dangerous for you. We need to buy food, and I have the money to pay for it."

As I spoke, my "armed" men walked back and forth in front of the window, giving Mr. Meksola an excuse for having dealings with us: he could say he had been forced at gunpoint to do what we asked. He seemed glad to do business with me, and we went back to the camp with bread, eggs, cheese, butter, honey, and a few chickens. A few days later, I led another group to the house of another farmer with whom I had had dealings. Again, there was no trouble, and we returned with more food. Each time we went out, though, we feared we might be seen and either ambushed or followed back to the camp. Our nerves were always on edge, and the supplies we brought back were quickly consumed. How long could we hold out in the forest?

One day while out gathering wood, I looked up and found myself surrounded by six partisans. Jankel Klerer had taught us to always be on the alert, and these men had stolen up on me without my hearing a thing. I recognized two of the men: Sever Rubinstein and Michael Loterstein. They had arrived in Kamionka on the run from Markuszow in May and had slipped out of town before the roundup.

The leader of this group of six was a Russian Army officer who had escaped from a German POW camp. His name was Tolka. He said that he had been exploring the area with the thought of establishing bases of operations for partisan activities when he came across a large group of Jews from

Markuszow. Sever and Michael were part of this group, and they had volunteered to serve under Tolka's command for this mission. I asked Sever if he could help us get some guns. He said he couldn't. They didn't have enough weapons, but there was a chance that the other Markuszow Jews, the ones hiding in Wola Przybyslawska Forest, might give me the names of farmers who would sell guns to our group.

The Wola Przybyslawska Forest was where the Warsaw Jew had wanted me to go when I first left Kamionka. It was a twelve-mile walk from our campsite. We could not wait for anyone to bring us weapons on a silver platter. I took two volunteers with me and, on my own initiative, set off through the forest. We had to pass very close to several small villages, so we had to always be on the alert. When we found the campsite with the people from Markuszow, we saw that they, too, were living in underground bunkers. I told them that Sever Rubinstein had said that they had connections with farmers who might sell us weapons. They said that they would go talk to the farmers; we should come back in a few days. When we returned several days later, they said that the farmers hadn't reached a decision. So again, they said that we should come back in a few days. The third time we went, we got the same answer, so I stopped returning. It was a long walk, and hard going. I had worn out three pairs of shoes. Klerer thanked me for making the effort.

FOR SOME REASON, I remember the date to this day. It was October 28, 1942, and I was out looking for dry wood when a man carrying a rifle appeared and asked me in Yiddish, *"Bist a Yid?"* (Are you a Jew?) I said I was and brought him back to the camp. His name was Sam Finkel. He was a Lithuanian who couldn't speak Polish well, and had wandered away from his group to see if he could find the Jewish camp he had heard about. He was one of the twenty-three Jewish POWs who just that day had escaped from Lublin. They became known as the Number 7 Lipova Street group because they had all lived in a part of the Lublin ghetto that was on Number 7 Lipova Street. They had been assigned to work in a German Army hospital where officers wounded on the Eastern Front were brought for treatment. Their main job was to clean up the officers and prepare them for examination by German doctors, but they were also charged with storing the officers' weapons and other gear in a special area. In early October, Pawel Dubek, who served as liaison between the People's Army (Armia Ludowa, or AL) underground and the POWs, alerted the POWs that they were going to be liquidated, so they decided to escape. They stole several rifles and pistols and, with help from the AL underground, made their way out of Lublin and into the forest.

After making his escape, Sam said, he had gone back to Lublin to get some pistols and had forced a German truck driver at gunpoint to drive him back out to the edge of the forest. He had a rifle. Desperately eager to get hold of a weapon, even if I had to steal it, I asked a couple of our young women to flirt with Sam and hold his attention so I could grab his rifle. But he kept the rifle on his knees and his hands on it the whole time he was talking. He told us his story in a matter-of-fact way, and then left. We didn't see him or any of the other POWs until midwinter of 1943.

As the days passed, we got organized. We all had our assignments. Some of us went out at dawn to gather fuel or steal potatoes from the nearby estates, where huge piles of potatoes were covered in straw, then by a layer of dirt, to keep them from freezing. Two others took buckets to the well at the edge of the forest to bring back the day's supply of drinking water. Others were assigned to guard duty around the camp and at the edge of the forest.

One cold November day, while I was on guard duty, I noticed some of our women walking off toward the villages. This was against camp rules, and I was amazed that nobody had stopped them. I was still on duty when they came back.

"How could you think you wouldn't be noticed?" I said. "All the villagers know each other and when they see a strange face, they start talking. You were putting all of our lives at risk."

As soon as I got back to our campsite, I called a meeting of our defense unit. I told the members what I had seen and what I had said and that I didn't intend to be captured and killed just because our women refused to abide by the rules. I said I was leaving and taking my cousins Froim and Usher with me.

The others were very upset. Avram Reis asked what they could do to make me stay. I had to think about this. Apart from making sure that the rules forbidding women to leave the forest were strictly enforced, what *could* be done? The only idea I could come up with was that our group should build a bunker of our own, for our own security. We would continue to guard the edge of the forest, but we would be independent and cook our own meals. I suggested that we build it on the east side of the road that cut through the forest from north to south. This made sense logistically, because we would be closer to the entrance to the forest. We took a vote. Approval was unanimous. That changed the mood. We were taking our lives as a unit in hand. We set to work immediately.

Blimka Lamberg and Esther Reis, Avram's niece, who were both seventeen, asked me if they could join us and help out with the cooking. Looking at them, I couldn't help thinking of my sisters. I said that, if it were up to me, I would accept them right away, but that I would have to ask my commander and the other men. When Jankel and the others approved, I told the girls that they would have to wait until we had finished building the bunker. It took us about a week. But then there was one more thing to do: bring in the straw we needed to sleep on. A friendly farmer told us that we could take as much as we wanted. We took as much as we could carry but first had to stuff it all into sacks so we wouldn't leave a trail.

On the third night in our new bunker, just before dawn, two of our men went to get water. They came running back. They had heard German voices down by the road. We always slept in our clothes, removing only our boots and jackets. As we started pulling on our boots, the two went back to investigate, while Usher, Froim's little brother, was sent off to alert the people in the main camp. A few minutes later, we heard a burst of machine-gun fire and the empty buckets of our two men clanging against the tree trunks as they ran back.

"Follow me," I said, and we all ran, with the machine-gun fire now continuous and grenades exploding behind us. I knew of a road that cut through the forest a few kilometers to the east. A strong wind had come up, bringing down dead limbs and branches. These forest sounds, together with the noise made by frightened animals that were also trying to escape from the gunfire, helped cover the noise we made as we ran. When we reached the road, we stopped and looked to see if it was safe to cross. About two hundred yards ahead, on the far side of the road, a three-man machine-gun squad was ready to cut down anyone coming out of the forest. We crawled on our bellies across the road, then ran for an hour, deep into the forest, until we came to a dense growth of thornbushes that tore our clothes as we crawled in. We lay there, listening to the machine-gun fire, which would stop and start again. It lasted for at least an hour. Then silence. The attack had begun shortly after daybreak. We stayed hidden among the thornbushes, afraid to move, until nearly midnight. Then, cautiously, we worked our way back to the camp.

Every bunker had been blown up. The doors had been blown out. Some of the men must have tried to rush out. Their bodies lay scattered around the campsite. We assumed that the others had died inside the bunkers when the grenades were thrown in. They hadn't stood a chance. In accordance with Jewish tradition, we buried our comrades immediately, dragging the bodies into the blown-open bunkers and covering them with dirt. Someone started to say Kaddish. We all joined in. No one cried. We swore that we would avenge the deaths of our comrades. We had walked only a short distance when the men suddenly hoisted me into the air. This was no time to celebrate, but I had sensed the danger and had insisted on building our bunker away from the main campsite, and we had survived.

We didn't return to our bunker, fearing that the Germans might be waiting for us. The next day, we came upon a group of a dozen of the campsite people, all young: ten men and Blimka Lamberg and Esther Reis, the two women who had planned to join us in our bunker. As soon as they heard the machine-gun fire, they said, they had run out of their bunker and gotten as far away as possible. We were all in shock. Seventy-five had been killed. Only twenty-five of us were left.

As we tried to figure out how the Germans had discovered the campsite, someone recalled having seen people in the forest who looked as if they were hunting for mushrooms. We concluded that they must have been Poles sent by the Germans to see if they could find where the POWs who had escaped from Lublin were hiding.

We had learned our lesson: it was dangerous to establish a fixed campsite, better to keep on the move, spending no more than one night in the same place, and, during the day, never remaining in one spot for more than an hour or two. We shared the hunks of bread we had in our pockets, and when our bread was gone we ate nothing. Food meant nothing to us. All that mattered was that we were alive.

THE WINTER OF 1942–43 was bitterly cold. We trudged through snow and sleet, slept on frozen ground, and woke up covered with a blanket of snow. We walked until we were too tired to walk, then lay down and tried to sleep. We went out on forays to steal potatoes from the big estates. One day as we were baking potatoes and warming our hands over the fire, I looked up and saw a boy I recognized. His name was Chaim. He was my age—twenty. He came from Michow, where one of my aunts lived. We used to see each other on Saturday nights when I biked over to visit her. We were both amazed to see each other here. He just happened to be going through the forest, on his way from one farm to another. He was hiding with farmers he had known from before the war. A Polish girl had offered to take him in if he would convert to Catholicism and marry her.

When he saw our pitchfork rifles and realized how badly we needed weapons, he told me that, a couple of years before, he had worked with a group of carpenters installing doors and windows in a house that a farmer was having built. One day, when they were all eating lunch together, the farmer boasted of having a big cache of weapons. And he said that he wasn't the only one. During the retreat, Polish soldiers had offered weapons in exchange for civilian clothes or had just thrown their rifles into the fields as they ran. So a lot of farmers had rifles that they had hidden away.

When Chaim finished talking, a chill ran straight through my body, from the top of my head down to my toes. A whole cache of weapons! The thought of all of us being armed, of being able to defend ourselves, was like a dream. I was so stunned that I asked Chaim to repeat everything he had just told me, word for word. The farmer's name was Lemeszek, he said, and he lived just outside of Michow. He gave me directions to the farm.

I went over to the others in our unit and shared the news with them. We had had leads like this before, but they had never worked out. I had the feeling that this time was going to be different and I said, "Tonight we're going to have guns." We paid Lemeszek a visit as soon as it grew dark.

Shortly after sunset, we walked out of the forest and across the fields to two farmhouses. The men shouldered their pitchfork rifles. I carried a broken, rusty handgun that I had "liberated" from a peasant. I was wearing a new ski cap and a policeman's sheepskin-lined blue overcoat—the gift of a farmer who gave us a whole load of coats and hats and uniforms that had been thrown away during the retreat. I had pinned a badge on my lapel, which made me look official, and I had grown a mustache to make myself look older. We commandeered sleighs and teams of horses and had the farmers bring us to Lemeszek's farm, which was about ten miles away. Chaim did not come with us.

On the way, someone asked who would be in charge of negotiating with Lemeszek. Klerer picked me and Shabse, who was broad-shouldered and tall and, with his bushy mustache, could easily pass for a Russian partisan in peasant clothing. He wasn't very smart but, unlike the rest of us, he knew one word of Russian: *Shto*, meaning "What?"

It took nearly two hours to reach the farm. We left the sleighs and their drivers under guard well away from the house. I led eight men to Lemeszek's door. I knocked. Lemeszek opened the door. He was wearing longjohns. He was as big as Shabse and didn't seem the least bit afraid of us. I spoke to him in Polish.

"Are you Lemeszek?"

"Yes," he said.

I shone my flashlight in his face, thinking this might intimidate him. It didn't work. He just asked us to come in. Then I shone the flashlight on my own face and on Shabse's so that Lemeszek could get a look at us. There was a bed in the middle of the main room and a wood-burning stove. Lemeszek sat down on his bed. I told him that we were paratroopers from Russia who had been ordered to organize partisan groups against our common enemy, the Germans. We had heard that he had a cache of firearms. I asked him to give them to us of his own free will; otherwise, we would have no choice but to use force.

Lemeszek didn't say a word and, again, showed no sign of being afraid of us. He just started to dress. When he had pulled on his jacket and boots, he said, "Follow me," and led us out to the barn. He reached into a bundle of straw and pulled out a rifle, which he handed to me. It was the first working weapon I had ever held. Then he went up into the hayloft, thrust his hand into the thatch of the roof, drew out a handgun and a bottle of bullets, and handed them down to me.

I handed the guns and the bottle to Jankel Klerer, who was waiting outside. But Lemeszek wasn't finished with us. He had another rifle, he said. It was buried somewhere, but he wasn't sure he could find it in the snow. A second rifle. We needed it. I was ready to try anything to get that rifle. I had rehearsed the act with Shabse. I pointed my flashlight at him. He glowered and straightened up to his full height, and, "*Shto, Shto,*" he said, looking grim. Then he grumbled a few nonsense words that were meant to sound like Russian.

Shabse had played his part well. Now it was my turn. I "translated." I told Lemeszek that he had to find the rifle no matter how long it took, because we needed every firearm we could get. The bluff worked.

Lemeszek picked up a shovel and an ax. Then, starting from the doorway, he took five paces straight out, stopped, turned left, and took another five paces. It took him a long time to chop through the ice and into the ground. Finally, about a foot down, there it was—a new rifle, coated with grease, and another supply of ammunition.

We were in for more surprises. Without any urging from us, Lemeszek led us to his neighbor, Pyotr, and repeated my story about our being Russian paratroopers organizing partisan units. I didn't have to say a word. Pyotr led us out to his barn, went up a ladder to the thatched roof, and brought out, one by one, a handgun, a revolver, and a few bottles of bullets. Lemeszek seemed to enjoy helping us. After we had left Pyotr's barn, Lemeszek told us about other farmers we might want to ask. They, too, had picked up weapons left behind by soldiers on the run from the Germans. We went to three of these farms. When we headed back to the forest, we had eight weapons. Finally, we could defend ourselves. It was a great moment in our lives — a turning point.

Chaim was gone when we got back. I never saw him again. He had appeared out of nowhere, told us where to find the weapons we desperately needed, and vanished. If we hadn't gotten those rifles, we probably would not have survived another week. It all seemed like a miracle — like my meeting with Mottele on the one night we both happened to be in Kamionka, when he told me how to find the campsite in the woods, offering me a better way to survive than by hiding with the Kloses. These chance encounters changed everything, literally saved my life, bringing me together with others with whom I could fight the enemy, instead of hiding alone and endangering the lives of those who sheltered me.

More than half of our unit had been in the army. Klerer set to work teaching the rest of us how to use our weapons. We went deep into the forest, practicing on targets nailed to tree trunks. After about a week of target practice, I came close to hitting the bull's-eye.

When we returned to the Michow area a week later, our first stop was at the home of one of the farmers Lemeszek had encouraged us to visit. He invited us in. After hearing my prepared speech, he said, "If you really are who you say you are, you should know who I am. My name is Zdunek, and my brother is a Communist and he's in Moscow. Why are you coming to me for guns? I expect the Germans to come after me any day now, and I'll need my guns to defend myself."

I hadn't expected anything like this. It took me a minute to come up with a reply. Making use of his own words, I said, "If you really are who you say you are, you should join us."

He thought this over, then went out to one of his warehouses, where he stored his grain. When he came back, he told us he had something for us, but we would have to get it ourselves. "It's right there, by the wall," he said. We went out to the warehouse and found a rifle leaning against the wall, as well as ammunition, and took it. Why he gave us the gun in this roundabout way, I have no idea. It was puzzling.

That night, we picked up four more guns. On our way back to the forest, we came to a house where a party was going on. We felt like celebrating, and several of us went in. The people were all young. They offered us vodka and kielbasa. We were having a good time when I caught sight of Zdunek standing outside, motioning me to come out.

He was furious. "For God's sake," he said. "You came here to get guns. Now get out of here because you're endangering all our lives. Some of these people could be collaborators. If they tell the Germans you were here, we could all get killed."

I went back into the house and told the others we had to leave immediately. Our hosts packed some food for us and gave us a bottle of vodka. They said they were sorry we couldn't stay.

We returned to the forest, wildly happy. Now twelve of us had guns, and we could protect the other thirteen members of our group. This included Blimka Lamberg and Esther Reis and the men who could not or would not fight, some because they were too frail, others for religious reasons.

CHAPTER III

FINDING ALLIES, KILLING COLLABORATORS

In January 1943, about two weeks after we got our guns, our guards spotted three Polish civilians, in their late twenties, carrying baskets as if they were gathering mushrooms—unusual in the middle of winter. We fanned out through the woods, watching them as they moved toward us, poking around in the leaves and then looking around and stopping to listen. When two of them got close enough to us, our men jumped them, but the third man got away, shouting, "Jews! Jews!" Then we heard gunfire. Though we couldn't see the shooters, we returned fire. We figured that German troops must have been coming up behind the Poles to provide support the minute they spotted fugitive Jews. We quickly disarmed the two collaborators, whose pistols, tucked into their

belts, had been concealed by their loose jackets. We tied their
hands, stuffed rags in their mouths, and made them run with
us away from the Germans, who had stopped shooting but
whose dogs were now barking. We kept on running until we
were out of breath, then listened, and moved on, the barking
now well behind us.

That night we asked a friendly farmer if we could use his
barn for a few hours and if we could have a couple of kerosene
lamps and pencil and paper. He asked no questions and said we
could have whatever we needed. In the barn, we separated the
two informers. Jankel and I interrogated one of them, while
Avram Reis took notes. First, we asked if they had been coming after us. He said no. Then I asked, if that was the case, why
were they walking through the forest with baskets pretending
to look for mushrooms at this time of year? The man mumbled
a few words that made no sense. So then I said, "Look, if you
don't start talking, I'll just shoot you." When he still refused to
talk, Avram worked him over with a potato masher. After that,
he began to talk. He admitted that he and his companion were
the ones who had led the Germans to the bunker site, that they
had been recruited by the Germans in May 1942, and since
then they had held meetings in villages around Kamionka at
which they represented the Germans and warned the villagers
that anyone who helped Jews would be severely punished. He
also admitted to encouraging young hoodlums to hunt down
and capture Jews, and also admitted to killing captured Jews
on whom they found valuables, telling the Germans that these
Jews had resisted arrest. Only near the end of the interrogation

did the first man admit that they had, in fact, been sent out to look for and capture any Jews who might have survived the blowing up of the bunkers.

I asked this man if he ever thought he would be captured by Jews. No, he said. Never. He always felt protected by "the German might." No Jew had ever resisted him or his partner before.

When we were done with the first informer, we questioned the second one. After starting out uncooperative, he gave the same answers to our questions. The information we got from our two prisoners was priceless. We learned that the Germans had a vast network of informers, with one or two agents in each village.

We took the two men with us to all the addresses they gave us, keeping them out of sight except when we needed to bring them forward to confront the collaborators. Some of the collaborators fainted when they realized who we were. We forced each confessed collaborator to lead us to others. We took six of them prisoner. Some of our men volunteered to execute them, as well as the two who had revealed the network. When they begged for mercy, I asked them what mercy they had shown our women and children. Those who had volunteered for the assignment carried it out. We felt that by executing these collaborators we were sending a message that those who helped the Germans murder Jews would be tracked down and killed. We also felt that, by disrupting the Germans' information network, we were carrying the fight to the enemy, and in this way were beginning to make good on our promise to avenge the deaths of our families.

Later that night, we traveled to the home of Boleslaw Dabrowski, a friendly farmer in Staroscin, a village between Kamionka and Wola Przybyslawska. We had rid the earth of six willing accomplices in the murder of our people and were in a mood to celebrate. Dabrowski provided us with vodka mixed with raspberry syrup. We drank much too much, ate all through the night, and were dead drunk when we fell asleep. The next morning, Dabrowski went to a grocery store in the village and heard that Jews had killed some collaborators. Word had spread fast; everyone was talking about it.

"Now I know why you were celebrating," Dabrowski said when he came back.

We had assumed that the mission of this network of spies and collaborators was to track down Jews who had gone into hiding. We soon realized that they had another assignment: to spy on the peasants—to find out if they were Communists or were selling farm products or slaughtering livestock illegally. That would explain why the people in some villages sounded the alarm when they saw us. They were afraid that the local spies would report them if they didn't immediately show their hostility. There were peasants who would gladly have taken Jews into their homes and passed them off as relatives if they hadn't feared that spies would denounce them and get everyone killed.

After spending the night at Dabrowski's, we no longer slept in the forest. We had gotten spoiled. We moved from one isolated farmhouse to another, walking ten to fifteen miles each night. Before choosing a farmhouse, we would scope it out, trying to find out how many people lived there. Then we positioned our men around the house so that anyone looking out a window would see one of us. That way, the farmer's family wouldn't be likely to make any trouble.

Klerer and I were the ones who went up to the door, with our rifles slung over our shoulders. We were always polite. We would usually say, "Good evening." And the usual reply was equally polite: "Gentlemen, how can we help you?" We then said we would like to have something to eat and a place to sleep. After that, we told everyone to come into the main room, and when they were all present, we tried to set their minds at ease by telling them that we had arrived through the fields without being seen or followed. We also said that if anyone tried to slip out and notify the Germans, he would put the lives of the whole family at risk, because we would defend ourselves to the death, and there was no telling who might get hurt in the cross fire. We didn't want anyone to get hurt.

After we had given our little speech, our unit would divide up, with some of our men sleeping and taking their meals inside the house and the others staying in the barn. We did this for two reasons: because there wasn't enough room for us all in the house, and because dividing up made it harder for our hosts to gauge our numbers. We liked people to believe that our unit was larger than it actually was. The amount of food we carried off to the barn helped foster this illusion. Our long night marches gave us tremendous appetites; we ate like wolves.

We would usually arrive in the dark and leave the next

night. Before leaving, we would remind the farmer and his family not to inform on us. Over time, some of our hosts became good friends or at least useful allies, providing us with information about collaborators and Jew haters in the surrounding villages.

Under the Occupation, every farmer had to contribute produce monthly to the Germans, who kept a record of his crops. When we took food, produce, dairy, livestock, and poultry, we signed a receipt, which the farmer could use as evidence that he had been forced at gunpoint to provide help. We were glad to sign receipts for far more than we had actually taken. The inflated receipts reinforced the impression that our unit was larger than it was, and it allowed the farmer to subtract the amount that he had been forced to give us from the quota of food that went to the Germans.

Moving around on foot in all kinds of weather, through snow and rain and sleet, was especially hard for the two young women who were with us—Blimka Lamberg and Esther Reis. We decided to build a hiding place for them, if we could find a farmer who would agree to take them. Leibel from Markuszow, the shoemaker's son, said he knew of a farmer in Majarka Kolony who might be willing to hide the girls. When the farmer agreed, we sent two men with Leibel to build the hiding place—under the planking of the barn, about four feet deep and roughly eight feet square. We followed slowly, wanting to give them time to finish their work before we arrived. One night, we found ourselves close to Dabrowski's farm and decided to spend the night there. The Dabrowskis prepared a meal for us and Mrs. Dabrowski asked if we had any laundry that needed to be done. We did, and we gave it to her, glad at the thought of wearing clean clothes for a change.

As usual, we split the group, with some of us going out to sleep in the barn, while Klerer, Avram Reis, Froim, the girls, and I slept in the house. Esther shared a blanket with her uncle. I shared my blanket with Blimka, who had given her one dress and her underwear to Mrs. Dabrowski to be washed, so she was naked. She was a beauty, but I did not touch her. But when I woke up—at dawn, because I was planning to meet Sam Finkel, who was coming over from the group in Wola Przybyslawska, early that morning—I must have brushed against her, because she woke up and kissed me with great fervor. This was completely unlike her. I could not respond, and I don't know that she wanted me to. I got up and pulled on my boots.

Reis was supposed to accompany me to the place where I had arranged to meet Sam, but Froim asked if he could come along. So then Reis offered to stay, and Froim and I left. After we had gone about a mile, we heard gunfire. When we turned to see where it was coming from, we saw smoke billowing up. Dabrowski's house was burning. A farmer was coming in our direction in a sleigh. I stopped him and asked him what had happened. German soldiers had surrounded the house, he said, and then they had set it on fire. Froim and I jumped onto the sleigh and told the farmer to take us to the edge of the forest as fast as his horse would go. Before we jumped down, we warned him not to tell anyone that he had met us. When we got to the place where I had arranged to meet Sam Finkel, nobody was there. We figured that he and his men had withdrawn when they heard the shooting.

Froim and I were deeply depressed by the loss of so many of our friends; we took it for granted that everyone in the house had been killed. We spent the night in a haystack and set out the next morning to meet Leibel and two other partisans who were staying at a farmhouse in Majarka Kolony, southwest of Kamionka, near Garbow, some twenty miles distant. We told them what had happened.

Two days later, Klerer and three other members of our unit turned up. We were amazed to see them. They had escaped through the back of the house. The others—Blimka and Esther, Reis and Shabse, the dentist Herschel and his brother, as well as five of the six people who lived in the house—had all been either shot or burned to death. Dabrowski had been executed; his wife had been spared. (In the 1980s, Yad Vashem designated Dabrowski and his family as Righteous Among the Nations. It was then that I learned the date of this event: January 31, 1943.) We concluded that Polish informers had trailed us to the house and alerted the Germans, who had arrived minutes after Froim and I had left at dawn.

We thought we had taken every possible precaution to make sure we were not followed. Now, we realized, our comrades had died as the result of our carelessness, our ignorance. We should never have stayed in a house that was as close to others as the Dabrowskis were to their neighbors. We had not taken sufficient care to make sure no one was following us or could track our movements. We decided that, from now on, whenever we left a farmhouse, we would start out together, but one man would then drop off to the side and remain hidden, watching to see if we were being followed. We would walk on for about a mile, then stop and wait for him to catch up and report before continuing. We avoided taking a direct route to our next destination; instead, we zigzagged through the fields, sometimes circling back on ourselves, doing everything possible to throw potential trackers off the trail. We were young. We were learning. And others had paid the price for our ignorance.

We stayed in Majarka Kolony for several days. Then one night in February, as we were walking from one farm to the next, we saw ahead a sizable group of men — ten or twelve — coming toward us. There was enough light in the sky to see their shapes, but not enough to see their faces or if they were wearing uniforms. We were armed. We ordered them to halt and identify themselves. They answered, *"Amchu,"* a Hebrew word meaning "We are your people."

I recognized Sam Finkel from our previous meeting, but I had never seen any of the others before. Like Sam, they were former soldiers who had escaped from the POW camp in Lublin. They had been hiding in a village outside of Wola Przybyslawska with a farmer named Drop. Their leader was Sam Gruber. Others in the group included Shlomo Eisenberg, Mikolai Berezin, Jusek Pisacki, Aron Gotz, Yosef Schengod, and five men whose last names I no longer remember: Furman, Cigan, Matros, Geniek, and Wladek. We took them back to the house in Majarka Kolony, where we shared our stories with one another — the loss of our families and our comrades. Then we discussed what to do next. Our unit had plenty of weapons; Gruber's group had only one or two guns. I promised Gruber that I would arm him and his men by using the contacts we had with the farmers who had given us our first firearms. It took us about a week, but we managed to acquire enough guns and ammunition and grenades to outfit Gruber's group. Gruber and the others all came from towns and villages east of the Bug. They wanted to return to their homes, to be reunited with their families. So we went our separate ways.

I CAUGHT A BAD COLD that winter. It got worse until finally I was running a fever and had a hard time breathing. Josef Hershman, the grain dealer's son from Staroscin who had many friends among the farmers, arranged for a sleigh to take the two of us to the edge of Kraszenin, a village a few miles north of Lublin. We then got down and walked, taking back ways until we arrived at a huge, solidly built farmhouse with a large barn, stables, and sheds. The farmer and his wife and their two teenage daughters greeted us warmly. The bond between Hershman and the family was clearly a close one.

As soon as the farmer learned of my condition, the two girls led us out to the big barn and up a ladder. They opened a trapdoor set into a false ceiling. Another ladder led to a room about ten feet wide and twenty feet long. There was nothing in it but two beds and another ladder. I lay down and the girls brought me hot tea and honey and a medication called *Kogotek*, something like aspirin.

Later, they brought me *Krupniok,* a peasant drink made of 190-proof alcohol, beer, and honey, served hot. They gave me only a couple of spoonfuls, and within an hour I started to sweat profusely. I sweated all night. Throughout the night, the girls washed me and changed my nightgown. Their care for me was unbelievable, unforgettable. I woke in the morning cured.

On the second day, one of the girls climbed up to alert us that two German gendarmes had stopped by and that her father had offered them lunch, but there was no need for us to be alarmed. We stayed there for three days, eating delicious pierogi and baked goods, drinking vodka, and enjoying the company of the delightful daughters. That the farmer and his wife allowed their girls to be with us up there in that hidden room alone, and to take care of me all night through, was testimony to their trust in us. Our stay was an incredible event in the midst of the war.

Josef Hershman was killed soon after he introduced me to this family, and I never went back to the farm.

IN MID-FEBRUARY 1943, Geniek Kaminsky, a member of the Polish Workers' Party, contacted us. There were four political parties in Poland at the time, each with its own fighting force: the Workers' Party, which the year before had organized cells of the People's Guard throughout Poland and later evolved into the People's Army, or AL; the Peasants Party, with its Peasants Battalions (Bechar); the Home Army, or AK (Armia Krajowa), many of whose members in the Lublin District were fiercely anti-Semitic; and the NSZ (Narodowe Sily Zbrojne, the ultra-

-nationalist, anti-Communist, anti-Semitic partisans who followed Nazi orders). Kaminsky had heard of our execution of the collaborrators. He had sent a message through one of the farmers who belonged to the Workers' Party saying that he wanted to meet us.

We met him in one of the villages south of Bratnik Forest. He was a round-faced man of medium height with light-brown hair. After congratulating us on our efforts to capture and punish collaborators, he explained that many of the same people who were informing the Gestapo about the whereabouts of hidden Jews were also betraying members of the Workers' Party and other anti-Nazi groups. He invited us to join the fighting arm of the Workers' Party, offering us firearms and support. When the time was right, he said, the party would lead an uprising against the Germans, and we could take part in it.

We thanked Kaminsky for the party's recognition of our efforts, but we did not commit ourselves to joining up with a man we had just met. We were wary of people who presented themselves as friends of the Jews. We had heard stories about how anti-Semitic Poles would betray Jews after winning their confidence by saying that they could help them in one way or another. We also felt that, if we joined up with a Polish group, we would end up being treated like errand boys. We told Kaminsky that we needed time to consider his offer.

About ten days after this meeting, thirty of us were traveling from one village to another in five horse-drawn wagons. There were some trees and houses about fifty feet off to one side of the road. Suddenly, shots rang out. Someone was shooting at the lead wagon. We all jumped down, spread out, and started to return fire, though it was hard to make out where the shooters were. The exchange of fire went on for maybe a quarter of an hour. Then we waited, listening, and heard people running. We ran after them, shooting as we ran. We killed two of them—we saw their bodies sprawled on the ground as we ran—and flushed out the others, who had tried to hide behind a couple of sheds. When they saw that they were outnumbered, they dropped their guns. We had expected men. These were just young punks.

Under questioning, they said that they were members of the AK, the Home Army. They had been ordered to kill us because we were Jews and because we robbed farmers. They said that their local leaders had received orders from London that no Jew should be permitted to survive to bear witness to the events of the war. We persuaded the punks to tell us who their leaders were. When we were done with our interrogation, we decided not to kill them because they were so young and we had suffered no casualties. We let them go, warning them that, if we caught them again, they wouldn't escape so lightly.

The next night, we paid a visit to the homes of the leaders whose names the hoodlums had given us. None of the men were at home, presumably because the hoodlums we had released had tipped them off. We left the message that we would be back. The fact that these young punks had been given the assignment to kill led us to conclude that the AK leadership underestimated our strength. If trained soldiers had been assigned to the job, it's unlikely that we would have survived the encounter.

Meanwhile, we had learned another lesson: to scout the routes we planned to take more carefully before setting out, and to determine, when it was still daylight, how to safely cross an area in the dark. Sometimes we scouted on foot; sometimes another partisan and I would commandeer horses to ride so that we could cover the terrain more quickly. We also began taking note of which direction houses faced and whether we could be seen from the windows. When we got back to where the others were staying, we drew up maps to use at night.

Slowly we were growing into our new lives as partisans. Many of us had come into the forest as boys with no experience of life outside of the shtetl, with no experience of living alone, of living in the forest, of having to steal to stay alive, and of killing another human. Except for those who had served in the army, we had never held a weapon. By acquiring firearms, we had taken the first step from being young fugitives on the run to becoming a guerrilla force in training. Now we were taking the second step: tracking down and picking up the spies and collaborators. Only then could we establish a base from which we could operate. At the same time, by going after the spies, who informed not only on us but also on the farmers and villagers throughout the countryside in which we operated, we changed the villagers' perception of us. They came to see us as a band of men whose mission was to kill German gendarmes and their collaborators and to avenge the death of any Jew. They also came to understand that if they tried to kill us or turn us in to the Germans, their own lives would be in danger.

In a world in which there was no justice for Jews, we tried to be just. If we were confident that somebody had killed a Jew, he would be killed. If anyone had beaten a Jew, he would be beaten. If anyone had verbally abused a Jew, he would get a severe warning. We had lost our faith in the God our parents had believed in, and had believed would save them in their hour of need, but we held on to our belief in justice.

IN EARLY MARCH, we contacted Kaminsky and told him we had decided not to join forces with the People's Guard unless we could operate independently. We were the only Jewish partisan group in our area and were already hooked up with the Markuszow group. We explained that we needed to retain our independence because we had to protect, feed, and provide shelter for Jews who were in hiding. At first, the answer was no: the party leadership had ruled that ethnic groups like ours could not operate independently, but must join either the People's Guard or the Russians. The reason was that the actions of one group could affect the lives and safety of others, and some guerrilla actions could do more harm than good. A few weeks later, however, Kaminsky relented: we would be allowed to remain all-Jewish and independent and could continue to protect hidden Jews, but would now be allowed to operate under the aegis of the People's Guard and carry. out joint operations with them.

It wasn't long before our relationship with the People's

Guard bore fruit. Kaminsky proposed a plan whose objective was to obtain more and better weapons than those we had acquired along the way. There was a castle in the region that served as a recreation and vacation center for Luftwaffe officers, who came there in shifts. The castle also served as an observation post for the air force. Kaminsky thought that we could get the weapons we needed if we took the officers and their security detail by surprise. We could disarm them and arm ourselves. He warned us, however, that the operation must be carried out without inflicting casualties, in order to avoid reprisals against the civilian population, especially the farmers who had helped us. He could provide a guide—a man named Kobala—and Kobala had recruited the castle's blacksmith, who knew the security routine: where the security guards' room was located, the route that the guard took when making his rounds, and so on. We couldn't carry out this operation now, in the winter; we would have to wait until the grain was tall enough to provide cover for our approach.

We were staying with a farmer in Michalowska Kolony— completely snowed in by a March blizzard—when I was involved in an incident that haunts me to this day. Our guns were precious to us; our lives depended on them; people were always trying to steal them. So I carried my pistol, a Polish Wis, attached to a chain hooked to my pants and tucked into the waistband. As I was pulling on my boots, my pistol fell out, struck the floor, and fired. The bullet hit a fellow partisan—Furman—who was standing nearby. The bullet killed him. I couldn't believe it. Furman was a comrade and a good friend, a casualty of my carelessness. From that day, I kept my gun in a holster, even though it took longer to draw the gun. Furman was the first person I had ever killed. For months, I had nightmares.

A few days later, while we were having dinner at a farmhouse, our host said he was hiding some Jews. I said I would like to meet them. He called for them and two men came into the room: Fiszel Wacholder and his father, Leble. I knew Fiszel, and I didn't like him. He had been a Judenrat policeman in Kamionka and was one of the Judenrat police who had tried to make me do fieldwork. I had refused and started to run up the ladder into the attic. When Fiszel came after me, I hit him on the head with a big Passover pot and ran off.

So now there he stood, this former neighbor who had wanted to turn me in to the Judenrat for refusing to obey his orders. If he had caught me, I might have been shot by the Germans as an example. Now he was at my mercy, but with his father standing at his side, a feeble old man who could barely walk. This was no time for settling scores. We arranged for the father to hide out on a nearby farm and took Fiszel, who was young and fit, along with us.

Not long after this, Yitzchak Morel, who was about six and a half feet tall, so he was easy to recognize, was on a mission to pick up food from a village with some other members of the Markuszow group. On the way back, he was riding in the rear of the last sleigh, straddling a CKM, a heavy Polish machine gun. He came from the region and had many friends there, so when two men came up alongside and called out his name, he thought it was just a friendly greeting. The two men quickly jumped up on the sleigh, killed Yitzchak and the other man, and took the CKM. When the farmer told us what had happened, we sent out scouts from the Markuszow group. They found the two bodies lying on the side of the road and buried them in Wola Przybyslawska Forest.

Through our own network of informers, we quickly found out who the killers were and went to look for them. As we started to surround their village, we were met by gunfire. We returned fire and set five or six houses ablaze, using incendiary bullets. Some of the shooters started to run away. We killed two or three of them as they ran. We then approached the home of one of the killers, with weapons drawn. His family said that the man we had come for wasn't there. A couple of days later, we learned that he was one of the shooters we had killed. The other killer apparently got away.

Toward the end of March—now a full five months after the deportation—we met the Lamberg brothers from Kamionka as they were walking through the fields. I asked them where they were coming from and where they were headed. They were just kids; the older boy was maybe thirteen. They said that they had been wandering around, spending one night at one farm, the next night at another. I asked where their parents were. They said that, before the deportation, they had made an arrangement with a local farmer. The Lambergs were a wealthy family, so the farmer could be sure that he would be well compensated. He agreed to hide the whole family and all their valuables. From time to time, the boys would go off to stay with other farmers in the area. One night, they came back to see their parents and were told that the Germans had taken them away. Since then, they had been wandering in the forest, not knowing what to do next.

We hadn't heard any reports of Germans in the area. So I decided to investigate. I asked the boys to tell me the name of the man who had taken in the family and where I could find him. Then I asked if they wanted to join our unit. They said no; they had many other places to hide. We understood; they were too young to fight with us.

A couple of days later, I took two men with me and went to see the farmer. As we approached the farmhouse, a dog started barking. Then the farmer's wife came out to the gate. I said I would like to speak to her husband. She said he wasn't at home and she didn't know when he would be back. I gave her my name and asked her to tell her husband that I just wanted to talk with him the next time we were in the area.

Two weeks later, we came back in the late afternoon, when most farmers fed their livestock. As we approached, I heard the dog barking again. And again, the woman said that her husband was not at home. I had the feeling that she was lying, so I asked if we could come in for some food. She said no, but I opened the gate anyway and we walked into the house.

Suddenly, we heard a man's voice screaming. The voice came from the attic, and the man was screaming for help. This seemed ridiculous since the closest farmhouse was several thousand feet away. I went to the bottom of the ladder leading up to the attic and told the man that there was no need to call for help. I just wanted to talk to him.

He started throwing down all kinds of valuable things — fur coats, silverware, and so on. I said I didn't want to take anything from him; I just wanted to know what had happened to the Lambergs. He refused to come down.

One of our men, holding a pistol, tried to go upstairs. The farmer fired a shot that grazed his finger. I sent a man back to our group for reinforcements. They came running and surrounded the house. I tried to talk the farmer into coming down. When he refused, we decided to smoke him out. We escorted his wife and children away from the house and drove the livestock out of the barn, whose straw roof could easily catch fire. We took a bundle of straw into the house and set it on fire in the front hall. It wasn't long before we heard the farmer coughing from all the smoke, but he didn't come down, so we lit a second bundle. The flames roared up and the thatched roof caught fire. We heard shots. The house burned down quickly and the truth of what the farmer had done to the boys' parents died with him.

We later heard that the farmer's wife had gone to the police and reported exactly what had happened — that we did not take anything from them, even the valuables, and that we only wanted to speak with her husband.

ONE NIGHT, FROIM ASKED ME if he could take a ride on a bicycle I had picked up. I gave him permission. Klerer and

I were leading the unit on a diagonal shortcut through Bratnik Forest—a path that was too rugged for a bike. Froim carried the bike out to the road, planning to meet us where the shortcut joined the road. As we came out of the woods, Klerer, who was just ahead of me, saw someone biking down the road with a rifle slung over his shoulder. Thinking it was a Polish policeman, he raised his rifle to shoot. I saw that it was Froim and knocked Klerer's arm aside. Klerer was a sharpshooter and the bullet would very likely have killed Froim. Instead, it hit him in the hand. We bandaged him and rushed him to our bunker at Drop's farm.

A few weeks later, we learned that Klerer had been killed. The news was a terrible blow. He and I had become close comrades in arms. Although he was older, he had never bossed me around and had always treated me with respect because of my knowledge and courage and because, he said, "you're not a show-off." He and his men had gone on a mission to "liberate" important labor-department books listing all the collaborators in the region who were on the German payroll. The books were kept in the Markuszow town hall, which was normally guarded, but not that night. German gendarmes and Polish police who just happened to be passing by had killed Klerer and one other partisan. Our men managed to bring their bodies back to base for proper burial. Our policy was never to leave our people behind, unless it was impossible to bring them away. Although we did not observe kosher rules and did not celebrate the holy days—except once, when we fasted for Yom Kippur—we always said Kaddish for our dead.

Gruber's men had found Drop and his farm in November 1942, when they regrouped after the Germans attacked them as they were making their way toward the Bug River, hoping to return to their hometowns. The farm was in the Wola Przybyslawska area and it was huge. Drop, who accepted payment in either zlotys or gold pieces, could hide as many as twelve people. Here was a place, finally, that we could use as a refuge for our wounded, like Froim with his wounded hand, and for those who were unable to travel with us—the elderly and the children. Among others who moved in here were Sever Rubinstein's brother, David; David's wife, Bella; and his sister, Blimka. Sever and I felt that they would be safer at Drop's than at the farm at which they had been staying.

Our ability to hide people who could not defend themselves depended to a large degree on people like Drop, gentiles willing to risk their lives and the lives of their families by taking in Jews and offering them shelter for extended periods of time. (Some of them were subsequently honored as Righteous Among the Nations at Yad Vashem.)

I went to Drop's farm regularly, together with a couple of our men, to supply food for the people in hiding. One day when Froim, whose hand caused him a lot of pain, felt well enough to go out for a walk, I took him out to Bratnik Forest to get some fresh air, and the two men who had come with me joined us. We stopped to sit under a huge oak tree that could be seen from miles away and which we used as a landmark. We were talking quietly when we saw four men walking in the woods. We were armed; they weren't. We told them to come closer. Then we saw that some were wearing POW pants, and we began speaking to them in Yiddish, the language we used among ourselves. They told us that they had been part of the group that escaped with Gruber and his men, but the group had been forced to split up when it was intercepted by the Germans, and some POWs had been killed. Like Gruber and his men, they came from east of the Bug and had been trying to get back to their homes. They were hiding in a farmhouse in Michalowska Kolony and paying the farmer.

They led us to their hideout, and there we met another seven or eight members of their group. Their leader, Marion Dworecki, was about ten years my senior—handsome, short, blond, and blue-eyed, a man who managed to look trim and neat even under the conditions we were all living in. He struck me as a natural leader. I told them about our unit—that it consisted of more than fifty men, that we were all armed, and that we kept on the move. I told them about our mistakes and our accomplishments, and they were impressed. In fact, as I was talking to them, it seemed to me that we had accomplished quite a lot.

Dworecki and I took a liking to each other, and I also got along well with his men. I asked them if they would consider joining up with us. They said that they would like to meet the other members of our unit and basically check us out before they came to a decision. So I brought them to our base and we all talked together for quite some time. Some of the men from the Markuszow group said that they didn't want to expand our unit. My feeling was that Dworecki—an army-trained demolitions expert—would be a great asset, and I argued that the two groups should merge. The Markuszow men kept saying no, until finally I lost my patience and said, "All right, if you don't want to expand, I'll join up with Dworecki." That turned them around. So our two groups merged and we armed Dworecki's men.

Not long after this meeting, Dworecki said that he wanted to go to town to "socialize" with the women, and wanted to know where our people would be spending the night. I was in charge of organizing our moves, where we would go and what route we would take, and I had made it a rule not to reveal this information to anyone who left the group even for an hour. My reasoning was that, if one of our comrades was captured, he would not be able to reveal our whereabouts even if tortured. My refusal to answer Dworecki's question made him furious. I got worked up too. I told him I wasn't going to risk the lives of all of our men just so he could have a good time, and that he must tell me where we could find him in case we moved out. He sulked and finally decided not to go. The next morning, he apologized for the words that he had spoken in anger and said he understood my position and agreed with it. After that, we became good friends.

A few weeks later, we passed at night through Michalowska Kolony, where Dworecki had hidden out. He said that he wanted to visit the farmer who had saved him, so I gave my permission. The farmhouse was right on the main road and had a side entrance. As we approached the house, I saw two armed men just leaving. I signaled to my men and we all dropped to the ground and took up defensive positions. We lay there for about ten minutes. When we could no longer hear the footsteps of the men who had walked out of the house, Dworecki and I stepped inside. We were lucky, the farmer said. The men who had just left were fascists; they were looking for us.

We had another narrow escape when I broke my own rule of never going to a hideout in daytime. One morning, I slipped through the wheat fields to Drop's farm in broad daylight to say hello to my cousin Froim and the others who were hiding there: David, Bella, and Blimka Rubinstein; a fellow named Hershel; and a young woman named Itka, whose three brothers were partisans, and Itka's little boy, David, who was about six years old. There was also a Hasid named Stefan Tuman. He had injured his foot in the woods while walking with the Markuszow group and was supposedly recuperating, but was not at the farm. When I was told that he had gone for a walk in the village, I was furious. As soon as he returned to the farm, I grabbed the pistol we had given him and smacked him with it on both sides of his face.

"How *dare* you take such a risk? Everyone's life is at stake and you go for a walk in the village in the middle of the day?" I said. "If your foot's good enough to walk in the village, you're healthy enough to rejoin us. That way, if anything happens, you can die with the rest of us." I gave his pistol to Blimka Rubinstein, whose courage I admired.

When I went back to the woods, Tuman came with me.

In April or early May of 1943, two of my comrades and I dropped in at the Klos farm. I had long wanted to pay

Mr. and Mrs. Klos a visit and thank them for their kindness at a time when I was most frightened and depressed. The Kloses and their children were overjoyed to see that I was alive. They embraced me as if I were a member of their family and told me that I was always in their prayers. They said that they were proud to see what I had become. They told me that they believed their prayers had helped me become who I was now—a confident man, a partisan. It was a very emotional reunion. I was finally able to thank them for what they had done for me. Their promise to hide me had given me the courage to escape going into the ghetto, and they had kept their promise. My comrades and I stayed for about half an hour. The Kloses offered us food and drink, but I didn't want to linger, fearing that our presence put their lives in jeopardy. So we took our leave and I told them I would see them again.

CHAPTER IV

THE RAID ON LESZEC CASTLE

AROUND THE END OF MAY, we began working more closely with Kaminsky and the People's Guard. When Soviet spies were dropped into our area, we were assigned to conduct them to wherever they were supposed to be. At the same time, we carried out many small-scale missions: ambushing German gendarmes, hunting down collaborators, and fighting local fascist groups. Our main area of operation was around Kamionka, Bratnik Forest, and the surrounding villages. I felt that we were now ready to do the job that we had been planning together with Kaminsky throughout the winter. This was the raid on Leszec Castle, the goal being to obtain as many weapons as possible without killing anyone. This would be our first guerrilla raid. Before carrying it out, we had wanted to scout the area thoroughly. We also had to wait until the wheat had grown high enough to provide cover as we moved forward.

We were excited about this first mission under the leadership of the People's Guard. Being young and armed, we thought we were invincible. It never occurred to us that we might all be killed.

Isser Rosenberg, commander of the Markuszow group, was in charge. He was a spirited and capable young man—another blond and blue-eyed Jew, unlike the German stereotype. He put me in charge of the forty-five men assigned to attack the castle once the guard had been taken care of. I was surprised that Isser picked me. I had no experience in this sort of operation. He later told me that Sever Rubinstein had admired my initiative and my refusal to give up when I made those three long hikes through the forest to the Markuszow group, trying to get weapons.

The plan was simple. One of the security guards patrolled the grounds every morning at about six. The blacksmith would give the signal that the guard had started on his rounds by a clang on the anvil. My men had crept up through the wheat field and were concealed about a hundred yards from the castle. Sever Rubinstein and Kobala, who were to disarm the guard, were much closer to the path that the guard patrolled. We were all in position, waiting for the signal. The blacksmith struck the anvil. We waited for the guard to appear, then waited for him to come close to where Sever and Kobala were hiding. We saw them leap up and heard them shout, *"Hände hoch!"* But instead of raising his hands, the guard tried to swing his rifle off his shoulder in position to fire. Sever then fired a shot into the air to frighten him. The guard raised his hands and they took his rifle, and Sever, grabbing him by the belt, led him away while my men and I ran toward the castle. As I was running, I almost bumped into a man who was dressed in a suit and a necktie. I asked him who he was. He said that he was the manager of the castle. I asked him if he spoke German. He said that he did, so I said, "Run with us," and he did.

When we reached the castle, my men took up positions around the building. We knew where the German security guards were: in the basement room with the barred windows close to the main entrance. I told the manager to tell the Germans that we had captured their guard and that, if they surrendered their weapons, we would not shoot. They were preparing to hand out their weapons when we heard someone inside the cellar say, *"Was? Waffen?"* (What? Weapons?) And then the command *"Feuer!"* (Fire!)

Suddenly, all hell broke loose. Several machine guns started firing out of the barred windows. The fire was so intense and sustained that trees were cut down just as if they had been sawed. There was no way we could throw grenades into those narrow, barred windows, so we pulled back, returning fire whenever possible. One of our men was wounded; otherwise, there were no casualties.

Although the operation—our first large-scale mission— could hardly be called a success, the experience made us eager to try again. Also, by capturing the guard and coming into close contact with the security detail, we learned that the enemy was vulnerable and didn't seem eager to fight until ordered to start shooting.

What happened next took us all by surprise. The following morning, through a villager who had dealings with the baron, we received a message: the baron had heard that one of our men had been injured and he was willing to provide assistance. He even sent money for medication.

A week later, we heard that the German garrison and pilots and the baron had moved off to Garbow, an estate south of Wola Przybyslawska that housed a distillery owned by another baron. We wanted to capture the Leszec baron because the manager had told us that he was a willing collaborator and that it was the baron who had ordered the Germans to shoot. The manager also told us that the baron wore a Luger, a high-quality German handgun—a sign that he was close to the Germans.

When we learned that all the Germans had gone, we again positioned men around the castle, and Isser and I knocked on the big front door. A butler opened it. When we asked to see the baron, we were told that he was gone, but his son was in residence. So we asked to see the son. The son came to the door and invited us in.

He was a good-looking young man, in his mid-twenties, dressed simply, no tie. His name was Yanuszek. He apologized for what had happened—one of our men had been injured— and said his father was not a Nazi sympathizer but couldn't refuse the Germans the use of his castle. He had no choice in the matter. After we had talked a bit longer, the young man led us over to the ceramic stove—a huge one that probably heated several rooms. He touched what looked like a cemented tile but was actually a hinged door. It opened. He reached in, took out a bundle of bills, and handed us 100,000 zlotys, or about $10,000. This was amazing enough, but he then told the farm manager to hitch up teams of horses for five wagons, and invited us to load up whatever we wanted—flour, cereals, grains, sugar, dried peas. It was all German property, he said. All he wanted was a receipt for whatever we took; he could use this as evidence that he had been forced to hand it over. We took more than we needed for our own use and gave a lot of it to the farmers with whom we were staying.

We still wanted to capture the baron. We wanted to talk to him, to find out how far he was collaborating with the Nazis. We took up quarters with a farmer about a mile from the castle. We had a pretty good idea of the baron's schedule. We knew that every day, at around noon, he came up from Garbow in his horse-drawn carriage, but on our way to the castle we saw a carriage driving off at full speed. When we asked if the baron was in, we were told he had just left. One of his staff must have seen us coming and warned him.

I asked the butler if the son was at home. He said that he was, so I asked to see him. I felt that the son had been lying to us about his father, and I told him so.

"You said your father cooperated with the Germans only because he had no choice," I said. "How do you explain the fact that this good man who opposes the Germans carries a German pistol? We hear that he socializes with the Germans, and not just because he's forced to. What I want you to do is send a messenger to your father telling him we want his Luger and ammunition and another hundred thousand zlotys."

The son said that he would do everything we had asked him to do. Before leaving, we noticed a sturdy saddle lying near the stable and helped ourselves to it. Then we told the messenger where he should meet us when he came to bring us the baron's reply. Before we even reached the forest, we heard hoofbeats and saw the messenger riding hard to catch up with us. He handed me the Luger, the ammunition, and the zlotys, but then very politely asked if he could have the saddle we had taken. It belonged to the son, not his father. We apologized and handed it over to him.

Later, we received a note from the son telling us that anytime we needed help or money we should send a messenger, and he would do what he could. And he was as good as his word. Whenever he got a message from Skinny Frank, he gave us what we asked for.

ONE DAY SHORTLY AFTER THIS, Isser Rosenberg asked me to accompany him to the Lukow estate, where he had traded in grain with the baron before the war. We had no reason to expect trouble but went armed with pistols and hand grenades. When we arrived at the castle, the butler opened the door and announced Isser's arrival. The baron greeted him, shook my hand, and led us to the dining room. On the way, he said, "I have a surprise for you, but don't be alarmed."

We entered the dining room and there, sitting around the

table, were about twenty-five uniformed AK officers. The baron introduced us as commanders of the Jewish partisan groups. The officers and men all stood up, a sign of respect. One of the officers said they had heard that we were good fighters, and they had looked forward to meeting us and hoped our groups could cooperate in fighting the Germans. They offered us a toast, and we all drank.

Later, the baron, who knew that we needed money to buy medicine for our wounded, left the room and came back with 100,000 zlotys. He handed the notes to Isser right there in front of the others, as if to prove to the AK that he supported us, as well as them.

We agreed to meet with the AK officers again and, after thanking the baron for his hospitality, left. On the road leading from the castle, we were approached by AK guards who had been posted behind the trees that lined the road. They greeted Isser warmly, with pats on the back, and invited us to join them in the village for a drink because one of the guards was celebrating a birthday. On the way to the tavern, I put my hand in my pocket and clutched my grenade. Speaking in Yiddish, Isser and I agreed that, if we sensed that the guards intended to kill us, we would detonate our grenades and blow ourselves up together with them.

We arrived at the tavern and were having a drink when one of the guards said that he would like to meet our entire group. That struck me as suspicious, but I said, "Okay. Come along," feeling that Isser and I would be safer with our men around us than here in the tavern.

The farmhouse in which we were staying was about five miles from the tavern. The guard whose birthday it was and a buddy of his came with us. When they arrived, they seemed surprised to see how many of us there were—about seventy at the time—and to find us all armed. They suggested that we all go out to celebrate the guard's birthday. After a quick discussion among ourselves in Yiddish, we decided that it would be a good move for some of our men to celebrate with them. To show our strength, we took about thirty men with us. Before we entered the village, we warned the two AK men that, if any shots were fired at us, we would torch the village. As a precaution, we lined the roads with machine guns. Isser, a few others, and I continued on our way to the tavern, where we had more drinks and celebrated the guard's birthday. The rest of our men remained in position and on alert. We didn't stay long. Before we left, the AK guards asked us to meet with them again and cooperate with them against the Germans.

No matter how friendly they seemed, we never trusted these AK people. We knew how anti-Semitic they were and that, if they could get away with it, they would probably kill us all. But this was our chance to show them that anyone who tried to harm us would have to pay dearly. We were a different generation of Jews. We had all been orphaned. We had been hardened by our life on the run. We would fight and we would kill. As it happened, however, the AK guards did not contact us after this meeting. Perhaps they had just wanted to see who and how many we were.

Later that summer, in June, Isser was killed—not by an

enemy but, tragically, by one of our own men. Several members of our group were staying at a farmer's house in Wola Przybyslawska. Michael Loterstein, Isser's best friend, was sitting across from him and playing with a revolver, which he thought was unloaded. He pulled the trigger and the instant he did so, realizing his mistake, tried to block the bullet with his hand. The bullet went right through his hand and struck Isser in the heart, killing him instantly. Isser Rosenberg—twenty-four years of age, handsome and brave, who never hesitated to take command and put himself in harm's way—had narrowly escaped death many times. Now he was dead as the result of a stupid mistake, the kind I myself had made when I killed Furman. I knew exactly how Loterstein felt. Again, we gathered to say Kaddish and bury a comrade.

SINCE WE HAD BECOME ARMED and organized, we had gone about our business—picking off known collaborators by twos and threes. The Germans quickly found replacements and came up with a fresh strategy. The new men were instructed to pose as partisans. They were armed with sawed-off rifles that could be concealed under their coats or jackets. They would enter a village and ask if any partisan groups were operating in the area. Once accepted into our ranks, they would find some means of letting the Germans know where we were so that they could surround us and kill us. That was the plan.

Our network of friends in the villages told us that two of these men had come around asking about partisan groups that they could join up with. We arranged to meet them near the edge of the woods. Our comrades were hidden close by, ready to alert us to any danger and protect us, if need be. When the two collaborators turned up, we talked for a while, and then I asked if they knew about the various partisan groups—the AK, the Peasants Battalions, and the AL. When they said that they did, I asked why they didn't join up with one of those groups.

"Why would a gentile want to join up with a group of Jews?" I said.

They couldn't come up with an answer. They could only stammer. Questioning turned into interrogation until finally I got the truth out of them: they were working for the Germans. We had a committee of six who served as our judges in matters like this. The sentence was death. The collaborators were shot and their bodies buried in the woods. Over the course of the next few months, our network of friends tipped us off to several more Poles who said that they were eager to join us, and then fell apart under questioning. They never had a chance to report back to their German paymasters. And the Germans could only guess what had happened to them.

It was around this time, too, that we learned that four Jewish men had been killed in a village northeast of Kamionka. They were POWs who had escaped from the Number 7 Lipova Street camp in Lublin. They had run out of money and been unable to pay the people who were hiding them. Local hoodlums had beaten them to death.

We told Kaminsky about the incident. He and two of his men accompanied us to the village where the Jews had been killed. We went to the house of the farmer who had hidden them and asked what had happened. He said that when the men told him they couldn't pay him anymore, he told them they would have to leave. When they left the farm, some hoodlums had paraded them through the village, beating them and spitting on them, and then beating them to death with clubs, in front of everyone.

We asked all the residents of the village to gather in front of the house of the village leader. Kaminsky gave a powerful speech. He explained that the enemy of the Jews was also the enemy of the Polish people. He told them that they didn't seem to realize what was happening: first the Jews would be treated like dogs, but the Poles would be next. Decent human beings do not beat other people to death.

When Kaminsky was done, we asked who the murderers were, and some of the peasants pointed them out. Kaminsky ordered his men to tie them up, and they were taken away. He told the villagers that the People's Guard would protect any Jew in hiding and punish anyone who victimized Jews.

Kaminsky was a party member but was not in the leadership of the partisan arm of the People's Guard, which by this time had become the People's Army, the Armia Ludowa, or AL. Now he introduced us to the AL commanders in the Lublin district: Miczyslaw Moczar, Franek Volinski, Jan Wojtovitcz, and Leon Marzenta. We had learned to be cautious, so, without the four commanders being aware of it, our men surrounded our meeting place and, well concealed, remained on guard until the meeting was over. We began to work closely with the commanders. They wanted to know all about the members of my group and about our contacts with farmers—which ones could be trusted. We also talked about strategy and tactics.

More and more German troops were now moving through the area on their way to the Eastern Front. The anti-Nazi Polish groups ordered their people to report all German troop movements; all the information we gathered was sent back to the AL. Meanwhile, it was not in the interest of any partisan unit to engage in a battle with German forces. They could always call in reinforcements; we could not. What we could do was attack and destroy German supply lines. This was ultimately more important to the war effort than killing a few Germans.

Later in the summer, we received orders to destroy three dairies. They were on the estates of Samoklesk, owned by Baron Kuszel, and Nasutow and Kozlowka, owned by Count Zamoyski. These estates, with their great grain fields and herds of cattle, were major suppliers for the troops engaged with the Soviets on the Eastern Front. We divided into three groups, each of which went to one of the farms and destroyed the equipment by tossing grenades through the windows. In Samoklesk, we found a Polish policeman on duty; we scared him off with a few shots in the air before blowing up the dairy. No one was guarding the Nasutow dairy, and we met with no resistance in Kozlowka. The destroyed facilities were quickly rebuilt, so we had to return and blow them up again.

IT WAS DURING THIS SUMMER—the summer of 1943—that my group of seventy-five men merged with Finkel and Gruber's group of about fifteen. Gruber was our senior member, and we all agreed that he should be given the command. Gruber and I worked closely together, planning operations down to the last detail. Our two groups complemented each other: Gruber's men had army training and experience with explosives; ours had access to weapons and greater familiarity with our area and its terrain. We shared a common goal: protecting Jews and avenging their deaths. It made sense to pool our resources and information.

Our numbers continued to grow as we came across other Jews on the run and invited them to join us. We integrated them into our group by training them and impressing upon them our belief that discipline and constant vigilance were essential to our survival. We were not formally connected with the command structure of the Polish and Russian partisans, and often had to take our own initiative without waiting for approval. If we had waited, we would have been wiped out. Our circumstances were entirely different from those of the Russians and the Poles. We could not disappear into the population; we did not have families and communities who could clandestinely provide support; and we had the added burden of protecting our people in hiding. Meanwhile, our informal association with the AL meant that we could request and receive intelligence information, firearms, and the explosives needed for sabotage operations. It also meant that we had access to the AL's network of couriers and guides who could lead us through territory with which we were unfamiliar. Many of the guides were peasant women, who were less likely to attract attention than men.

The farmers who lived along the road from Lublin to Chelm now reported to us on enemy movements along the road. They said that German convoys were starting to pass through in an endless stream, and that the convoys usually consisted of eight or ten trucks preceded by two motorcycles with sidecars for machine gunners. We decided to attack only those convoys accompanied by the motorcycles, figuring that these convoys were probably carrying vital supplies. This kind of operation would represent a far greater challenge than lobbing grenades into dairies.

We staked out positions along the road where there was some cover—shrubs and bushes—and got down into the drainage ditches that lined the roads. About four feet deep and eight feet wide, they made good trenches. We spread out, with eight or ten men in each position, about two hundred feet apart. The first group's job was to take out the machine gunners on the lead motorcycles. When the trucks behind them slowed down, we used the machine guns and anti-tank guns we'd gotten from the AL, aiming at the gas tanks so the trucks would explode. When we were done, the roads looked like *gehenom*, real hell, with flames and black smoke billowing up.

Sometimes a truckload of security troops would bring up the rear of the convoy. As soon as they realized the convoy was in trouble, they jumped off the truck; our machine gunners were waiting for them. We did not pursue them if they managed to make their way to the ditch on the far side of the road because we would have to expose ourselves to fire. Our strategy was to hit and run. When a large group of men was needed for the strike, we had wagons and teams of horses concealed at some distance from the road so that we could get away fast.

THAT SUMMER, WE PLANNED a strike into Kamionka. As a deliberate insult, the Germans were using our shul for their offices. We decided to burn it down. As a youngster, I had watched the workers build the shul and excavate the basement, pushing the wheelbarrows back and forth across the town square, taking the dirt out to the meadows. I was thrilled by the thought of marching into my hometown with my fellow Jewish partisans and carrying out this operation.

We went directly to the shul. While some of the men prepared to break in, open the doors, and pour gas on the wooden floors and file cabinets before setting it on fire, German soldiers stationed on the rooftop of the school building spotted us in the town square and began shooting. We returned fire with our one machine gun. The shooting stopped, and we went on with our work. We knew that Polish police were stationed in town, but they must have kept to their barracks. We never saw them.

As the building caught fire, a man ran toward the square, shouting, "Jews! Jews!" He must have thought that our men were Polish policemen. He ran right into Shlomo Eisenberg, who grabbed him and brought him to me. I recognized him immediately. This man was a collaborator notorious for his viciousness in rounding up Jewish girls who had escaped the ghetto before deportation and were hiding with farmers. We had heard that he would strip them naked and parade them through the village streets before handing them over to the Nazis. I told Eisenberg to tie him and keep an eye on him. We took him with us.

As we were making our way back to the forest, we could hear the church bells and the fire alarms of Kamionka in the distance, but we were not followed. Later, under interrogation, the collaborator told us that the Germans had praised him as a "good Jew hunter" and rewarded him with sugar and produce for turning in Jews or killing them if they had valuables. After he confirmed that he was indeed responsible for the acts that had been reported to us, we killed him.

WE SPENT THAT NIGHT at a farm north of Kamionka. After we had packed up and left and had gone a few hundred yards from the house, one of our men realized that he had left a bundle of ammunition behind. The next evening, we sent two men back to retrieve it. When they failed to return quickly, I took a few men with me and went to see what was going on. I found our two men, the farmer, his laborer, and the maid all searching for the missing ammunition. The farmer said that he had no idea where the ammunition was, but the laborer, with my Luger in his face, admitted that two men on bikes had come by earlier and taken it, and that he knew who they were: they were friends of the farmer's younger son.

I told the farmer that I would be back in two weeks to pick up our ammunition. If it wasn't there, he would have to pay one thousand zlotys for each missing bullet. I figured we had fifty or sixty bullets in our package. He assured me that I would have my ammunition.

Two weeks later, I returned to the area with my men and took quarters at two farmhouses several hundred yards apart and about a mile from this man's farm. My plan was to pay the farmer a visit the following afternoon. Dworecki's group had taken up quarters in one house and my group in the other, which was near a wooded area.

Late that afternoon, as we were eating our evening meal in the farmyard adjoining the woods, the farmer's wife walked up to me and asked why we had arrested her husband. I told her I didn't know what she was talking about. She left, and fifteen minutes later, she came back and asked, "What did we do wrong? Why did you have my husband arrested?" This time, I asked her what made her think such a thing.

"He left a horse to graze in the woods," she said. "Today, he went to bring the horse back, and I haven't seen him since."

I immediately felt uneasy. I grabbed my rifle and got up to hide behind the trunk of a tree, a huge tree, nearly five feet in diameter. I lay flat on the ground. Fiszel Wacholder got down beside me, and I ordered the others to spread out and take defensive positions, facing the woods.

As dusk approached, I could see figures moving through the trees. Thinking it was our men coming to join us, I yelled, "Dworecki? Matros?" The reply came in a burst of machine-gun fire. If Fiszel and I had not been behind that tree, we would both have been killed. We all fired back. The gunfight lasted about ten minutes. When it quieted down, we pulled out, having suffered no casualties.

Again, it had been a very close call. If we had taken the footpath to meet our comrades in the next house, we would have been caught in the ambush and wiped out. The AK had made a big mistake: they had kept the farmer from returning home, fearing that he might give away their presence in the woods. If he had come home, his wife wouldn't have asked me what we had done with him, and it was her questions that made me think something was wrong.

Two hours later, when we joined up with Dworecki's group at our prearranged meeting site, we tried to figure out who had tried to ambush us, but neither of us had any idea who it could be.

The next day, we stopped at a beekeeper's house. As we approached the house, our men deployed in the usual formation. I asked the beekeeper's wife if we could have some honey. She had just gone off to get a jar when Shlomo Eisenberg suddenly appeared, shoving a man into the room. He said that the man had jumped out of the attic window.

I asked the man who he was and why he had tried to get away from us.

"I'm not guilty," he said.

"Not guilty of what?" I said.

Finally, he admitted that he was a member of the AK and had been involved in the ambush a few days before, when we were having our late-afternoon meal. He said that two AK groups had been holed up—one at the wealthy farmer's house, the other at his older son's house nearby. They had been waiting for us to come back to retrieve the ammunition that our man had left behind. He gave us the names of the leaders of the group and said that there were a lot of men in it, maybe as many as thirty.

About a week later, we surrounded the older son's house and captured and interrogated him. He admitted what we already knew: that half of the AK men had been stationed at his place, the other half at his father's. We tied his hands behind his back and took him along to his father's house, to make sure nobody would shoot at us. Along the way, we asked him if the AK unit was still at his father's house. He said that he didn't know. When we came near his father's house, we deployed our men around it. Matros, Rubinstein, Romek, Laks, and thirty or so others remained in the meadow with the son, while Dworecki, Eisenberg, and I entered the house. We found the same three people as before: the farmer, the laborer, and the maid. The farmer insisted that he was innocent; he said that his younger son was the cause of all this trouble, that the son now owned the farm, and he was helpless to stop him.

Under questioning, the frightened laborer and the maid confirmed that the AK had stayed in the house for more than a week, that they were armed, and that they were friends of the younger son. We ordered them to remove all their possessions from the house and get the livestock out of the barn. Then we set fire to both structures. We did not harm the old farmer and we released his older son—they had told us the truth—but we decided that we had to burn down his home to show the villagers that we would punish anyone who collaborated with those who plotted to murder us.

It took us a full year to track down the men responsible for the failed ambush, including the farmer's younger son. We didn't kill him because we hadn't suffered any casualties and he showed remorse. His excuse was that he was a member of the AK and was only following orders. This was credible, because we were outside of the area in which the AK group with which we had reached an informal understanding operated. On the other hand, we were all aware that any understanding arrived at with the AK was only a temporary truce, made for purely strategic reasons, in what was a relentless campaign to kill Jews and prevent the AL and other leftist groups from coming to power after the war.

About a month after this incident, the leadership of the AK sent a message through Kaminsky asking us to meet AK party members—politicians, not soldiers—at the home of a prosperous farmer in a nearby village. The agenda was to discuss what the AK believed was senseless killing on both sides. I invited two AL officers to accompany us to the meeting: I wanted their presence as evidence that we were not acting entirely alone, but with the blessing of the AL. When we got there, the AK party members wasted no time in launching a tirade against us. "You are living off our people, the Polish people," one of the party members said. "And you are killing them. *You have no right to murder Poles!*"

"Who are we killing?" I said. "We are killing people who murder Poles and Jews. I am a partisan, and if I come to your house and ask for food and you try to shoot at me, I will shoot back. You kill Jews simply because they are Jews, and you kill them even when they are unarmed!"

Another AK member supported me. He said that we were all partisans and we all had the same objective: killing Nazis. Then the spokesman suggested that we make a deal: if any AK men attacked us, instead of killing them, we should turn them over to the AK, and it would determine their punishment. In turn, the AK would hand over to us any Jews who, in its opinion, deserved punishment. I asked the obvious question: "How can I bring you a person who shoots at us unless he's dead?"

They conceded that I had a point there. The discussion continued until we reached an agreement. The AK party members asked us to promise that we wouldn't shoot at them unless we were shot at first, and we agreed. It seemed to me that they had finally come to understand that we would kill anyone who killed Jews, including other partisans. After this meeting, there were no more ambushes or killings of Jews in the area in which we were operating, between Lublin and Kamionka, including Bratnik Forest.

My men and I were quartered with two families who lived in adjoining farmhouses in Siedliska Kolony, close to Kamionka. We arrived at about nine in the evening, and asked for food and shelter. The peasants fed us and served us drinks, and then, as usual, some of us went out to sleep in the barn, while others stayed in the house. Even in the house we slept on straw on the floor because there were no cots.

At about nine the next morning, my cousin Froim woke me. "Get up," he said quietly. "Germans."

I was on the floor near the front door, opposite a window, with another window in the wall to my left. I got up, pulled on my boots, and saw a German gendarme — a sergeant, carrying a rifle slung over his shoulder — walk past the window. He turned the corner, so I saw him again, through the second window. I had no time to think, but I realized that if he looked in, he would see sleeping men sprawled on the floor, their weapons close at hand. I had my gun in my hand and was standing behind the door by the time he opened it.

"Good morning," he said in Polish. I shot him in the head. He fell backward. Back in Kamionka I had been so afraid of the Germans that I couldn't look them in the face and kept my eyes on their boots. This was the first time I had killed a German at close range. I felt no regret. I felt only the satisfaction of having avenged the murder of my family. I took his Luger and a rifle.

A German officer who had heard the shot opened fire on the house with a submachine gun, hitting Eisenberg, who was up in the attic, in the shoulder. All the other men grabbed their weapons and charged out after the shooter. Mikolai Berezin was the first to come around the corner of the house, looking for the German. The German had grabbed hold of him just as Froim, following Berek and with his rifle at the ready, yelled at the officer, telling him to put his hands up.

Surprised and confused, the German released Berek and, still holding his submachine gun, pleaded with Froim, in Polish, not to shoot. Froim shot him in the stomach. He fell backward, just like a tree chopped down in the forest. Others shot him again and again to make sure he was dead.

When the shooting was over, we turned around and saw, parked in the driveway, a car that took our breath away: a brand-new, blue-gray Opel Olympia sedan. We ran over and opened the doors. It was packed with all kinds of supplies: eggs, butter, cheese, honey, and, best of all, ammunition magazines filled with bullets for the submachine gun we took from the dead gendarme. Then the question was, what to do with the car?

None of us knew how to drive. Even if one of us had known how, we wouldn't be able to buy gasoline or oil. So we took axes and hammers and pickaxes and pounded the car into scrap metal.

After tending to Eisenberg, we left the two bodies where they lay and headed back into the forest by horse and wagon. About an hour later, Germans surrounded the village, searching for us. Luckily, one of the neighbors told the Germans that the partisans who had been in the house spoke Russian; this was so that the Germans wouldn't blame the Poles and make them suffer for something they had no part in. When the Germans heard that Russians were in the area, they collected their dead and left.

ONE PERSON WE WERE EAGER to settle accounts with was a fellow named Braslow, the manager of the Zamoyski estate at Kozlowka. This was the estate in which I had spent my first night in hiding, the night before my family was deported from Kamionka. Braslow had served as a captain in the Polish Army during the war; after Poland surrendered, he had joined the AK. We heard that he was boasting that no Jew would dare to raid his count's castle; any Jew who tried would be carried out dead.

We made our plans, and one night, a group of forty-five Jewish and twelve AL partisans, commanded by Leon Marzenta, surrounded the palace. We got close without firing a shot. Then we cut all the telephone wires, and three of us walked up to the main door with our guns at the ready and knocked. When the butler opened the door, we said that we wanted to speak to Mr. Braslow. The butler said he wasn't in. We said we would search for him, and the butler admitted us and led us from room to room. We spent about half an hour searching the bedrooms, the library, the living room, and all around the castle. There really was no one there except the butler and the house staff.

We told the butler that we were hungry. He asked what we would like for dinner, and after giving us a tour of the kitchen and a look at all the food in the huge iceboxes, he had the staff prepare a royal meal for us. We posted some men on guard duty and ate in shifts. Everyone had his fill. At around midnight, we went to the stables and barns, where the grounds-keepers and grooms lived, and asked them to hitch up three wagons. We loaded the wagons with white flour, sugar, barley and buckwheat, honey and beans. Whatever the count had was under German control, so we took what we needed and more. Following our usual practice, we shared our haul with the farmers in the region who had helped us.

It amused us to think how Braslow, who had boasted that any Jew who tried to raid the count's castle would be carried out dead, would react when he found out that Jews had dined in his dining room and carried out wagonloads of supplies without a shot being fired.

CHAPTER V

RUSSIAN AIRDROPS AND SABOTAGE MISSIONS

By August 1943, all the groups in our area were ready and eager to take the fight to the enemy, not just engage in skirmishes with German gendarmes or a gang of hoodlums. But we needed to be better armed and to have more credible intelligence than we had been getting so far. We knew that the AL was working closely with Russian partisans and the Russian government, and that it had access to Russian weapons. Stalin had told his generals that anyone willing to fight against the Germans should be given all the help they needed: firearms, intelligence information, and so on. With the AL's pledge of support, we now felt able to carry out sabotage missions.

A few weeks later, AL headquarters ordered us to go to a

clearing in Parczew Forest called Ochoza; it was expecting an airdrop of Russian firearms, which would be distributed among the partisan groups. We passed through several AL checkpoints on our way to the clearing. Hundreds of partisans were converging on the area. When we finally reached the clearing, we could hardly believe our eyes. A whole arsenal of first-class, modern weapons was being distributed: anti-tank guns, mortars, mines, explosives, machine guns with magazines on top that held seventy-two rounds of ammunition, submachine guns, and medical supplies. Our allotment was three anti-tank guns, six machine guns, and thirty-two submachine guns, as well as ammunition, grenades, and explosives. We loaded our supplies on wagons and took off as fast as possible. We couldn't carry everything, so we stored some of the ammunition and grenades with friendly farmers, who by this time felt engaged in the fight against the Nazis. Now we were equipped to carry out serious sabotage operations.

Through the AL, we learned which of the trains on the Warsaw-Lublin line carried military supplies to the Germans fighting on the Eastern Front. Then we asked AL headquarters to provide ten or twelve men to help us carry out our first serious sabotage mission. We wanted them to take part in this action alongside us because, no matter how friendly things seemed on the surface, we remained suspicious of Poles, even Polish partisans. The AL's willingness to send these men to share our risks would go a long way toward reassuring us. They sent us the men we requested.

We scouted the area to see what security measures the

Germans took, find the best place to set the charges and blow up the train, and plan our escape after completing the mission. We picked a spot near Moticz and deployed our men at nearby intersections to secure the roads that crossed the tracks in order to prevent an attack from the rear. Dworecki, our demolitions expert, needed six men to place the mines on the tracks, with their wires connected to the line that led to the detonator, about a hundred and fifty yards from the tracks. I was in charge of securing the area and the logistics of pulling out as soon as the mines blew up.

The tracks were regularly monitored by German guards on hand-pumped wagons, each equipped with a strong searchlight to scan the rails and sidings for signs of trouble. We observed that they came about half an hour ahead of the supply trains, which passed by at roughly two-hour intervals. That half hour was all the time we had to place the explosives, so everything had to be done quickly. We waited until the locomotive was on top of the first mine, then Dworecki pushed the plunger, which set off all the other explosives. The locomotive rose into the air in a burst of smoke and flame. The freight cars buckled and slid off the tracks. The air was full of burning debris that came clanging down all down the line. More explosions followed as other mines went off and as ammunitions and explosives blew up. The night sky was bright for half a mile around. It was for me—for all of us—an unimaginable, unforgettable moment. We had blown a Nazi train sky-high. It was a dream come true, and over the following months, it would be repeated time and again. However, the Germans were as efficient at removing the debris and repairing the rails as they were at killing Jews; service was usually restored within forty-eight hours.

A few days after we had blown up our first train, there was an incident at Skrobow, the site of a POW camp. German guards from Lubartow and Lublin used to come to villages like Skrobow in groups of two or three to spend an evening with young Polish women. Using two Polish women as decoys, we ambushed four drunk Germans, whom we killed and whose weapons we took. AL members helped us get rid of the bodies in the forest, covering the site with leaves and brush, hoping to prevent the Germans from executing villagers in reprisal. The Germans might guess, but they would never know, what had happened to their four men.

It was at around this time, perhaps mid-September, that we learned that on September 9, a unit of the Polish National Armed Forces (NSZ fascists and Jew haters) had killed twenty-six Jewish partisans in Borowa Forest, south of Lublin. They had gained access to the partisans' base by pretending to want to help them, then had come at night and thrown grenades into the bunkers while the partisans slept.

The AL later composed a beautiful song in memory of those partisans, but the words fail to mention that the partisans were Jews. "On the ninth of September, everyone should remember when the NSZ stabbed the People's Army in the back," one of the lines goes. Throughout the war, songs were written and sung in Russian, Polish, and Yiddish in the base camps and hiding places throughout the forests. They helped to boost our morale. They made a lasting impression. More than sixty years later, I still sing them.

Later that fall, the AL sent us to Lubartow; our orders were to steal the labor-department books showing payments to collaborators, which were kept in the town hall. This was the same kind of mission in which Jankel Klerer had lost his life in Markuszow. Headquarters provided us with a female guide. She led us to the town hall, walking well ahead of us and alerting us to the presence of patrolling gendarmes by speaking to them in a raised voice. This time, no guards had been posted and we were able to steal the books without incident.

Around the end of December 1943, high-ranking Russian and AL officers requested my presence at a meeting to be held in the village of Bojki, on the edge of Parczew Forest. I took my close friend Sever Rubinstein with me. Our meeting with the officers lasted three days. We discussed strategy and future operations, and we ate well and drank well.

On the last day—in fact, the last day of the year, December 31—three farmers arrived from Huhnin, a village that was also close to Parczew Forest. Huhnin was the hometown of a fellow named Kolka Mieluch, a member of the AL staff. The farmers told Kolka that seventy German soldiers had occupied four houses in Huhnin, while their commanding officers had taken quarters in the nearby town of Ostrow-Lubelski. "How could you allow so many Germans to come here into our backyard?" they asked.

Kolka turned to me, Sever, and two AL members and asked

us to go back to the village with the three farmers so that they could show us which houses the German soldiers were occupying. After we had identified the houses, Kolka and the various high commanders of the AL drew up plans to organize a group of around fifty men under the command of Russian and AL officers, myself and Sever included. We were to disarm but not kill the German soldiers if possible, to avoid Nazi reprisals against the villagers. We were divided into four groups; each group was assigned to one of the four houses. The firing of a white flare was to be the signal for the attack. We hoped to take them all by surprise to avoid casualties. However, as we approached the village, a guard saw us and opened fire with a machine gun. At the same moment that we returned fire, the signal flare was sent up, and seeing the signal, each group set off toward its designated house. The German guard dropped his machine gun and ran off.

Sever and I were in the group led by Kolka. As soon as we had taken up defensive positions around "our" house, he ordered the Germans to come out with their hands up. There was no reply. So Kolka told them that, if they didn't come out, we would burn them out, and we started to collect bundles of straw from the barn to place around the house. Kolka then tossed a hand grenade over the roof to scare them. The sound of the explosion, together with the sight of the straw being brought up, did the trick. The soldiers opened the windows and jumped out of the house and raised their hands. They had left their weapons behind. Other units employed the same tactics at the other houses. The whole operation took about fifteen minutes and yielded a large arsenal of weapons: machine guns, submachine guns, pistols, hand grenades—all Russian-made. Only one of us was injured, but the soldier who shot him was killed instantly by one of our men.

We were in for a surprise: these German soldiers weren't German. They had Asian features and black, silky hair. They were Russian-speaking Muslims, former Red Army soldiers who, after being captured on the Russian front, had volunteered to fight with the Germans rather than remain in POW camps. When we searched them, we found maps of our area and evidence that, the day before, they had carried out a raid on partisans not far from where we were.

Our Russian commanders, coming face to face with men who had switched sides and joined up with the Nazis, demanded that they be killed on the spot. So the Russians and the AL fighters marched them out of the village and into a wooded area and executed all the soldiers except their officers. The Russians wanted to interrogate them before killing them.

Shortly after midnight, we headed for the area where the Muslim soldiers and their German officers had carried out their raid the day before, thinking that it would be a safe place to make camp. Around 9:00 a.m., we felt the ground trembling and, looking through binoculars, saw German tanks surrounding and attacking the village of Huhnin. There wasn't anyone to shoot at. We had warned the villagers to leave.

The Russians marched the six Muslim officers off into the woods and executed them, using silencers. By this time, our scouts had moved out, ready to alert us in case the German forces started to move in our direction. They observed the Germans collecting their dead and heading out of the area. Later that night, we returned to Bojki with our newly acquired arsenal and then returned to our quarters in different villages.

Until the end of January 1944, we continued with our search for collaborators and our hit-and-run sabotage missions. Then, in the first week of February, the AL informed us that another well-armed Jewish partisan group was based in Parczew Forest. It was under the command of Yechiel (Chiel) Grynszpan.

Sever Rubinstein and I traveled on horse and wagon the forty or fifty kilometers to see him and found Chiel, with his brother Avram and some other men, at a farmer's house in one of the villages near the forest. Everyone greeted us warmly, except Chiel himself. He was aloof and unfriendly. His men fed us and gave us something to drink, but the conversation was stilted because Chiel just sat there and never said a word, while his men made excuses for him. He liked to drink. He could have just been getting over a hangover.

THE MOST IMPORTANT MISSION of my years as a partisan took place in mid-March, when Leon Marzenta and I were given a special security assignment by the AL command. By this time, our group's relationship with the AL was solid: they treated us as equals; we had won each other's respect and were friends. Still, we remained on our guard.

Our assignment was to protect, to the death, the four most important members of the Krajowa Rada Narodowa (KRN), the underground, Communist, pro-Soviet Polish government-in-exile, and to bring them over to the east side of the Bug River. From there, they would be flown to Moscow, to the Soviet high command.

The men were Osobka Morawski, who later became the Polish prime minister (he subsequently wrote about the journey in his memoir but never mentioned the Jewish partisans who protected the group); Major Marian Spychalski of the AL; Dr. Jan Haneman, a member of the KRN and the Polish Socialist Party; and Kazimierz Sidor, a partisan from the Lublin district and a high-ranking AL leader in the Parczew region. His brother, Staszek, and his sister, Stephana, were also partisans there.

Lieutenant Marzenta and I each took five men. We moved from village to village and from one farm to another, always heading toward the river. AL guides worked with us and the AL security on both flanks and the rear, something we had never seen before. We understood then that, as the innermost circle of defense, we were ultimately responsible for these leaders' lives and that failure to protect them could affect the lives of millions. At the time, it did not occur to me that there was anything strange about the fact that we, a group of six Jews, had been picked to take part in this mission. Perhaps the fact that we had survived against all odds and could be counted on to fight to the death had something to do with their choosing us.

It took little more than a week to reach the Bug River, and during that time my men and I became very friendly with our charges. The future prime minister was our cook and loved to sing with us after lunch. The camaraderie was genuine, and one day Morawski even invited me to come with him to Moscow. I was flattered and thanked him for the invitation but declined. I needed to be with my men. He understood that.

When we reached the last rendezvous point on the west side of the Bug, we moved into a farmhouse and waited for a courier to let us know when to set out for the riverbank. He arrived around midnight. He told us that we had to be at a designated site, where three rowboats would be waiting, by 2:00 a.m. Then he handed us over to another guide.

We made our way to the riverbank and spread out to provide security. Some flooded areas along the riverbank had iced over, and as we slogged along, I sank through the ice and had to be pulled out and helped up onto the shore. By the time we reached the rowboats, my pants and jacket were coated with ice.

The men waiting for us on the other side whisked Morawski, Sidor, and the others away. We were ordered to go to the nearest village and wait there for new orders. To provide quarters for us, all the villagers had been evacuated into the forest, except for one man who came back to bake bread. When we entered his house, we found the oven heated, ready for baking. I hung up my clothes in front of the oven and stood before it for an hour, in my underwear, shivering, trying to thaw out. I had my backpack with me, but it had gotten soaked, too, so I had nothing dry to wear.

Our host brought some straw for us to sleep on. We rested

for several hours, until two couriers arrived. They told us that a Hungarian unit attached to the German Army was quickly approaching and that we should head to the forest to join up with the Voroshilov Russian partisan group. My clothes were still damp and stiff. I managed to pull my boots on but couldn't button my uniform jacket. I threw my coat over my shoulders and ran out into the cold.

The map we had been given proved useless. We trudged through the woods until almost midnight. Finally, a Russian voice told us to halt. After we had identified ourselves, we were led to the Russians' campsite deep within the forest. It was a huge camp, with an excellent trench defense system, at least twenty miles east of the Bug. Several thousand heavily armed partisans were encamped there. They were housed in hundreds of little shacks. We were invited to enter one of them. It was so crowded that there was no place to sit. One of the AL men that I knew invited me to sit on his lap, so I did—and immediately started itching and scratching. I had picked up lice.

After the Russians shared what information they had about the advance of the Hungarian troops, our twelve men were divided into three groups and integrated into the larger company. I was assigned to a group whose task was to ambush a Hungarian unit at the edge of the forest at 4:00 a.m. We stood in the cold for six hours but saw no action.

When our replacements arrived, we returned to camp. I needed a shave, so I hung my mirror on a tree and was about to lather my face when machine-gun fire erupted behind me. We all grabbed our guns and ran for the trenches, but by the time we got there, the shooting had stopped. Later, our commanders told us that a platoon of Hungarian soldiers had been killed. At about 2:00 p.m., it started snowing heavily and we stomped around trying to keep warm. That evening, after several feet of snow had fallen, we received orders to abandon our positions. We were given guards and guides who led us to a Polish partisan unit, the Wanda Waszylewska Brigade, named after a Polish Red Army war correspondent.

I was soaking wet and aching with cold when, through the trees, I saw people standing around a huge cauldron hanging over a roaring fire. I got as close to the fire as I could and sat there on the ground for several hours, trying to get warm and dry out, but when I finally got up, my clothes were still damp. We stayed in that camp for more than a week. Then a courier led us to two rowboats that were waiting to take our unit and some other men back across the Bug. One of those men was Jurek Pomeranc, my future brother-in-law, who proved to be an outstandingly courageous partisan.

Once we were on the other side, we were on our own. We headed west on foot and found a farmer a few miles from the river and asked him for something to eat. He happened to be Ukrainian and answered in his language, *"Omechka."*

I asked Jurek what the word meant, and he said it meant farmer cheese and sour cream. We asked for some bread and milk to go with it, and to this day, when my wife, Cesia, prepares a similar dish for us at home, I remind her that we are eating *omechka.*

We continued to move westward. By that time, I had lost

the gilt buttons from my uniform jacket, and since we were close to towns and villages, I asked a villager where we might find some. He directed me to a teacher who had been an officer in the Polish Army. He thought that the teacher might have a few buttons to spare. That night, accompanied by a couple of my men, I went to see the teacher in his second-floor apartment. While we were up talking to him, our guards posted on the street warned us that somebody was moving around a block or two away. We wanted to find out what was going on, so we left the apartment and called out in Polish, "Who's there?" Whoever it was opened fire. We returned fire. When things quieted down, we walked down the street and found a horse and wagon loaded with food and an ammunition disk for a Russian machine gun. We were glad to take possession.

In the next two villages we approached we ran into men from Chiel Grynszpan's group and learned that it was one of his men who had shot at us, mistaking us for AK. We returned the ammunition to him. His name was Leon Lerner. He was among the first prisoners to kill an SS officer during the revolt at the Sobibor death camp, in October 1943. Today he lives in Jerusalem.

Chiel's men had grim news to share with us. While we had been away on our mission, crossing and recrossing the Bug, eight fighters from the Markuszow group had asked Sam Gruber for permission to return to their area for a few days. He had granted permission. It appears that on their way toward Markuszow, they failed to follow the protocol that Gruber and I had established. This required that any house we chose to stay in must be isolated, that the area around the house must be secured and a guard posted, and that no family member be allowed to leave the house until twenty-four hours after our own departure. Germans had surrounded the house, stormed in, and killed them all, sparing only the Polish family. The death of these courageous men was a terrible blow. Losses due to carelessness were doubly painful.

Once we were back in the Parczew region, we linked up with the rest of our unit and headed for the Kamionka-Markuszow area. We had just entered a village called Serock, north of Kamionka, when two AL liaison officers warned us that there were Germans in the area. They urged us to evacuate immediately. Ten minutes later, we had everything loaded up on two horse-drawn wagons and were racing to reach the River Wieprz before the Germans could catch up with us. We waded and swam, holding on to the thick ropes we had strung across the river, and were ready for the Germans when they arrived on the far bank. We were determined to prevent them from following us across the river, so there was a fierce firefight. It lasted several hours. As we moved off to the north, our machine gunners kept the Germans pinned to the far side of the river. When Romek, one of the Number 7 Lipova Street POWs, was wounded, they provided cover for Eisenberg, who ran out and brought Romek out of the line of fire. Without those machine guns, we would never have survived.

We sent two men ahead to commandeer several horses and wagons and to bring them to the edge of a small woods. We pulled back slowly until we reached the wagons. Then we jumped on and told the drivers to get us away as fast as they could. Later, we went on foot into a deep forest. The next day, requisitioning other horses and wagons from other farmers, we traveled through the night to Parczew Forest.

A few days later, we returned to the Kamionka area. On our way, we had to cross a bridge, which, we saw as we got closer, was guarded by two Germans. We observed them from a distance until we had established that there were no others, just the two. A couple of our men then stole up through the fields close to the bridge and surprised the guards. They told the Germans to raise their hands and drop their rifles. They were older men, in their fifties, and one of them said, "Do whatever you want with us. Just don't leave us here, because if you don't kill us, the SS will."

We felt sorry for them. They seemed like decent men. We took them with us.

IN MID-APRIL 1944, two AL officers—Jan Wojtovitcz and Francziszek Volinski—arrived at our camp near Bratnik Forest. They brought news from headquarters: the Russians were planning a major offensive. It was essential that our group join forces with Chiel Grynszpan's group in the Parczew region. I hadn't forgotten the way that Chiel had treated us the last time we met, but we had no choice. We needed the kind of support that only the AL could give us. Volinski told me that the AL kept a file on all the partisan groups and had put together reports on virtually every partisan, including where he came from, his performance as a fighter, and so on.

The AL appointed Chiel commander of both groups. Sam Gruber was second in command, Marion Dworecki and I became platoon commanders, and all of us were promoted to the rank of first lieutenant. I initially declined, uncomfortable with the idea of being in command of men who were older than I was. I was just twenty-one. But Gruber urged me to accept the appointment. He told one of the AL officers that I knew more about tactics than a lot of men with years of military experience, and the officer recommended that I be given an assistant with the military training I lacked. The man he picked for the job was a former sergeant in the Polish Army named Moishe Peltz, from Markuszow. I accepted the command.

Two days after we received our commissions, I walked into the village. I wasn't wearing my officer's stars because I didn't like the idea that comrades older than I was would be required to salute me. But when my AL commanding officer saw me, he ordered me to wear my stars. From then on, I always did.

During April 1944, the Wehrmacht and SS, under the command of General Lippmann, moved into Ostrow-Lubelski. They used the town as a staging area for raids into Parczew Forest. When Wojtovitcz and his group passed through the area, the Germans opened fire on them and a battle began. A Russian named Janowski and his group, coming from Jedlanka, were moving into the same area. When they heard the shooting, they got out their field glasses to try to make out who was who. When they saw the German uniforms, they came around from behind and opened fire, forcing the Germans to retreat, after suffering casualties.

About a week later, the Twenty-seventh Division of the AK, which had been based in Volyn, east of the Bug River, crossed over to our area in Parczew Forest. The AL and Baranowski's Russian group warned the men not to attack the Jews; to do so would be considered a hostile act—a declaration of war against the AL and the Soviets. Within a few days, the division found itself surrounded by Germans. Couriers were sent to request reinforcements. The couriers found Chiel's group.

Chiel notified the AL command, which sent eighty men from its ranks and Chiel's to assist the AK. The message described exactly where the AK was and where the Germans were. Attacking the Germans from the rear, the partisans forced them to withdraw. Some Germans were killed in the action, and some AK men were killed as well; neither the AL nor Chiel's group suffered any casualties.

After that battle, the AK agreed to cooperate with the AL, although without any formal joining of forces. It was understood that, at least for the duration of the war, the two groups would stop fighting each other and the AK would stop killing Jews.

The intelligence we got from the Soviets and the AL was that the Germans were preparing to clear the area of all partisans in advance of the expected Russian offensive. The last week in April, we received orders to bring all of our men to Parczew Forest by May 1. The four of us who had received our commissions—Chiel Grynszpan, Sam Gruber, Marion Dworecki, and I—were then summoned to the village of Bojki, on the edge of the woods, where General Rola-Zymierski, head of the AL for all of Poland, had convened a three-day May Day conference for the AL leadership and the Jewish partisans operating to the north and northeast of Lublin.

The general confirmed that the Russians were planning a major offensive across the Bug River. He advised us, Polish and Jewish partisans alike, not to leave the area under any circumstances, because we would be needed to help establish the postwar Polish government after the war ended. He also warned us that we faced the risk of being caught between the advancing Red Army and the retreating Germans, in which case we should scatter and conceal ourselves in groups of two or even singly. He ended by emphasizing that we must remain within the area, no matter what difficulties we might encounter.

When the formal meetings were over, General Rola-Zymierski asked if he could inspect our forces. I had no idea how to prepare our men for an inspection, and Gruber was too busy to help. But my new assistant, Peltz, knew exactly what to do. Peltz got our quarters and our men in as good shape as could be expected of a partisan unit. Two hours later, the general arrived, inspected us, and expressed his approval. Knowing that we were all Jews, he asked if we knew what had happened to our families and if any of them had survived. He was not surprised when we responded that they had probably all been murdered. "I understand," he said, and I believe he did. He struck me as a refined, intelligent man, and I think he was genuinely moved by this meeting with a band of Jewish partisans.

He awarded medals in recognition of our courage in battle; the local AL had given him the list of names. It was a deeply moving experience, especially for those of us who had been just boys when we left our villages and went into hiding. Now we were truly part of the partisan movement, on an equal footing with the AL and the Soviets. Now when we had to go through checkpoints in villages, the partisan guards knew who we were and treated us with respect.

During the conference, we discussed strategy and began to gain some perspective on this great war in which we were involved, but of which we knew very little beyond what happened within our own region. We heard for the first time that the Russians had been gradually pushing the Germans back, reclaiming territories that the Germans had seized in 1941. There was hope in the air.

On May 3, Rola-Zymierski said goodbye, wished us luck, and left. The following day, we were told to prepare to move out, but were not told where we were to go. Then, on May 5, we were ordered to assemble in Jedlanka. Chiel, Gruber, Dworecki, and I met to discuss what to do with the people in our family camp in Parczew Forest. We couldn't take them with us, that was clear, and we couldn't leave them behind, where they might be found and killed. We asked the AL commanders — Moczar, Wojtovitcz, and Volinski — if we could leave some of our men with them, to protect them.

They understood the need, and they agreed to our request. Their response came as a great relief; if they had refused, we would have had to disobey their orders and protect the families on our own. They told us to figure out how many men we would need to protect these people. We decided that Chiel,

Gruber, and Dworecki should stay with their group and protect the camp, while my platoon, under my command, would go with the AL to Janov Forest, south of Lublin. I was chosen to lead because I knew the area better than the others. Janov Forest was chosen as our destination because the state of Lublin had been designated the site of the newly established Polish government once the area was liberated. The new government would require security forces to preserve law and order.

On May 6, we were one thousand three hundred strong in the village of Jedlanka, near Parczew Forest. Roughly 5 percent of the people within the staging area were women — Polish AL women, Jewish partisan women, and Russian partisan women. A small percentage of them fought alongside the men; the majority helped with the "housekeeping" chores — preparing meals, washing and mending clothes, caring for the sick and injured, and so on. Their assistance was indispensable.

Our new fighting force was led by Brigadier Commander Alexander Skotnicki, whose nickname was Zemsta (Revenge). Miczyslaw Moczar was the supreme commander, Wojtovitcz and Volinski were captains, Leon Marzenta and Kolka Mieluch — a Ukrainian and an anti-Semite — were lieutenants, and all were members of the command staff. The force included AL groups, a medical team, the Wanda Waszylewska group, the Holod Battalion under Gustaw Alef-Bolkowiak, a Russian group of three hundred under the command of General Chepiga, and my unit of forty-five men. There were two battalions from the "Poland is not yet lost" group, Baranowski's Soviet group, Czerny's group, and the Janowski group.

We had one hundred horses with wagons carrying provisions, arms, and ammunition. Several wagons were used as field kitchens. Anyone with a Russian submachine gun was given from five hundred to one thousand rounds of ammunition to carry. We had fifty scouts on horseback.

Skotnicki, who was a Jew, had picked Jurek Cholomsky, who had proved to be an outstanding fighter, as his guide, and Jurek had received permission to take his girlfriend, Roska Duman, with him—a sign of Skotnicki's high regard for Jurek as a man and as a fighter.

We left for Janov Forest that same evening, marching alongside the horses and wagons on unpaved roads leading south. That night, we covered almost seventeen miles to a village named Wandzin, near the Kozlowka Forest. We camped there during the day, and that night we marched to Dabrawa, another village near the edge of the forest, and then moved into the center of the forest, where we stayed for two days.

On May 7, as anticipated, the Germans stormed Parczew Forest, expecting to find thousands of partisans—and found no one. The family camp was well hidden, on an island in the middle of a swamp. The Germans did not go anywhere near it. So they left and asked the Luftwaffe to fly reconnaissance missions over the region. The pilots spotted us about five miles southwest of Kamionka, in Amelin. As the woods there were thin, we were unable to fully conceal our horses and wagons. They gave us away.

At dawn on May 10, the Nazis attacked. We had dug defensive trenches and were well prepared; the Germans, suffering heavy casualties, could not dislodge us. At one point in the fighting, a small airplane came in to pick up a wounded German who we figured must have been a high-ranking officer. We suffered no casualties. The Germans pulled back. Before we moved out, and after asking permission from an AL officer, I sent a messenger to the baron's son, because I knew that we would need money for medications and supplies. Always reliable, he sent back 200,000 zlotys.

On May 12, fully aware that we remained in the sights of the German command, we moved under cover of darkness from Amelin toward Rablow, a distance of some fifteen miles on our trek south to Janov Forest. The sun was rising when we arrived in the village, and I could see the dew sparkling on the meadows. Then something caught my attention: it seemed that the only people in the village were either very old or very young. This seemed odd to me, but it wasn't the sort of thing that I felt I could bring to the attention of a superior officer. It just made me wonder if the villagers had been warned that partisans were on the way.

Rablow was a tidy little village, with a strip of woods to the southeast and a meadow to the southwest. My platoon was at the head of the troop column. Because I was acting as a guide for the other commanders, I deployed some of my men through the barns and a few of the farmhouses, and I stayed in one of them. We also set up a camp in the woods, with field kitchens nearby. Then we notified our superior officers where we were and tried to get some sleep.

I stretched out on the floor of a farmhouse and was sound

asleep when, at about eight that morning, Lonka Pfefferkorn, our most reliable reconnaissance scout, rode up on horseback, entered the house, and shook me awake. He handed me a written order from Brigadier Commander Skotnicki. My orders were to send out six of my men, on the double, along with several other partisans, to set up an ambush for German columns approaching from Lublin. The message came with enough lead time for all of us to dig in and prepare ourselves for battle. Lonka was standing by my side, awaiting my signature on the orders, when suddenly a German plane sent a burst of machine-gun fire through the roof and into the floor about three feet away from us. The floorboards sprang up, shattered by the impact of the bullets.

Half-dressed, I grabbed my boots and machine gun and ran out of the farmhouse with Lonka and saw that several planes were circling the village. I also noticed that our camp kitchens were engulfed in smoke, and I figured that our kitchen fires had given us away. Then I saw Lonka's horse — a big, handsome white horse — cropping grass by the doorway, and I realized that the pilot must have spotted it and thought someone important was inside the house: a target worth strafing.

Four or five planes were now flying above us, and I ordered my assistant to send out men to carry out the ambush order. A few minutes later, however, our commanders ordered everyone into the woods, where two officers assigned us all to different areas. The wooded area we were in was roughly rectangular, about one thousand five hundred feet wide and three thousand feet deep, enabling us to create three lines of defense.

Meadows extended on three of its sides, while a section of the village, which was built on higher ground, formed the fourth side. Our view was of the backs of a row of houses, about three hundred yards away.

My group dug in on the north side. The trenches we dug weren't the kind used in trench warfare but were long enough to stretch out in and deep enough to provide cover for us and our equipment. The machine gunners' trenches held two men: the gunner and the loader. Looking around, I saw that the woods were now completely filled with our forces. The three hundred Russians under General Chepiga were to my right. Twenty or thirty of his men were disguised in German uniforms so they could slip across the line, if necessary.

The next order we received was to recall the men who had been sent out to conduct the ambush, because the German soldiers were slowly encircling us while the Luftwaffe started bombing our positions. The planes came in so low that they seemed to be scraping the treetops. The bombs brought trees crashing down, killing several of our men. We were so well organized that we were able to quickly remove and replace a fallen fighter with another from the next line of defense. Our orders were to hold fire until we could see our target clearly, rather than shooting wildly.

One of our officers shot three flares in the air—white, blue, and red—which might have confused the German pilots into believing that their ground forces were signaling them to stop the bombardment. In any case, the planes disappeared from the sky.

A few minutes later, the Germans laid down a barrage of rifle and machine gun fire all around us. They weren't close enough to see us, and none of our people were hit, so we assumed that the barrage was designed to force us to pull back. We stayed put.

I was observing the houses in front of us through my binoculars when suddenly, I saw Germans running out of them toward Chepiga's men on my right. My first thought was that these were his disguised partisans, the ones wearing German uniforms. When I looked again, I saw that the soldiers were running and ducking, and I knew that Chepiga's men would not have moved this defensively. I sent a runner to find out what was going on. He came back with word that General Chepiga and his force had already pulled out of the area. I was shocked. I told the runner to inform headquarters, positioned in the center of the forest, that reinforcements were needed. It quickly gave orders to send men to secure Chepiga's spot. As they moved in, the ten or twelve Germans who had begun penetrating Chepiga's side of the forest were killed, and the line was secured.

Several minutes later, the German troops, which we later found out included units from the Viking SS stationed in Lublin, started to storm our positions. We opened fire whenever we could see them and the full battle began. I was running back and forth, making sure that our machine-gun loaders had enough ammunition and looking out for wounded men who needed medical attention, when I heard a terrible scream and saw Romek fall. He was badly wounded, his hip blown out by the concussion from a bomb. As he lay, moaning and writing in agony, I sent somebody to the command center to bring a medic, but there was no way to save him. Jan Wojtovitcz put him out of his misery. I could not look. Romek was a dozen years older than I was; he was Sam Gruber's age — a good fighter, a fine human being, valiant to the end. To those who have never been in such a situation, shooting a dying man may seem an inhumane act, but we knew it was far less cruel than letting him suffer excruciating pain with no means of relieving it, much less of saving his life.

We fought the Germans at close quarters in a battle that lasted until nightfall. At no point did any of our men panic. They held their positions and showed great courage and discipline. The Germans sent in wave after wave of men, but we were well dug in and cut them down before they got near us. There were some instances when an enemy soldier was killed and others came in to pray over the body. We assumed that these soldiers were Muslims, like those we had encountered in the village of Huhnin.

One of the two Germans who, weeks before, had been guarding a bridge and had joined our unit proved his loyalty to us in a remarkable display of courage during this battle. When he saw that our men had killed a German machine gunner, he ran forward, grabbed the machine gun, returned to our trench, and started firing at the Germans.

Finally, realizing that they could not dislodge us without reinforcements, the Germans pulled back. We had been prepared for the worst, determined to fight to the last man, and had anticipated heavy casualties. But it was the enemy that suffered heavy losses, both dead and wounded—in the hundreds. We lost thirty men, with another twenty-five wounded. These were the great German forces commanded by the notorious Viking SS troops who were under orders to shoot any German soldier who retreated under fire. And we had held them off. More than that, we had forced them to retreat.

We buried our dead and took our wounded with us as we began to pull out. We had been instructed that, at nightfall, we should disperse in whatever direction we could, regrouping later at Bojki. So now we moved out in different directions.

This was the biggest and fiercest battle I had experienced. (When Gruber and I went back on a visit to Poland in the 1980s, we met with General Mietek Moczar, head commander of partisan forces at the Rablow battle. He told us that, after the war, the Polish government had formally set aside May 11 as a day of commemoration for Rablow, the most important partisan battle against the German forces of the war. When General Moczar died, in 1986, he was buried on the grounds of Rablow. We subsequently learned that, soon after the burial, a gang of fascists dumped wagonloads of manure on his grave.)

We needed to get away from Rablow as fast and as far as we could and find suitable cover. We walked all night. Near dawn, we entered a young forest where the terrain was as level as a tabletop. That night, five hundred men slept there.

The next morning, an AL scout reported that hundreds of German reinforcements, including tank columns, were approaching Rablow. We were ordered to move out, again, as fast as possible. My men and I were still sleeping when we got the order, so we were the last to leave. There were fifteen men in my group, and by the time we reached the edge of the forest, there were no guides left to tell us where to go. We decided to head north, to our home base in Bratnik Forest. On the way, we stopped at a farm and had a stroke of good luck. One of the women was in the midst of preparing cheese pierogi. She gave us some, as well as sour milk and bread fresh from the oven. We then asked her husband to give us a lift in his and his neighbors' wagons to the fields and farm roads farther north, near Markuszow. So now we were back in our own territory, but we were on our own.

As we approached the main railroad line from Warsaw to Lublin, we saw a train carrying tanks and German soldiers, and ducked into the wheat fields until it passed. Several hours later, we arrived at Wola Przybyslawska and let the farmer return home. Another farmer gave us a ride to Bratnik Forest. That night, we went to see the local farmers who had given us lodging before. We stayed with them for several days, resting up after all we had been through.

To find out what was going on, we sent one of the woman couriers to Bojki. When she returned, she told us that she had run into Kolka Mieluch, the Jew-hating lieutenant from the AL, and that he had ordered us to come to Bojki on the double. I had the feeling I knew why Kolka wanted to see us: he wanted our machine guns. And I was not about to give them up. So I took Sam Finkel and Felusz, a gentile from the AL, and the three of us rode off to Bojki on bicycles. When we arrived, we were told that Kolka had gone on to Jedlanka, but he wasn't there either. In Jedlanka we were told that he was in the Ochoza area, waiting for an airdrop of firearms from the Russians. So that's where we went.

There, we found bonfires burning in the sign of an M in a large clearing—the usual signal for the Soviet airdrops. We could hear the planes flying overhead but couldn't see them. While we were waiting, Staszek Sidor, a Polish partisan I had gotten to know when we crossed the Bug, warned me that Kolka was bragging that he was going to disarm me. So my hunch was correct, and I was glad I had not come alone. The parachutes began to come down around us. Along with the firearms airdropped that night came 110 paratroopers, some of whom got hung up in the trees. They wore Polish uniforms and were under the command of Major Klim, a tall, good-looking man in his fifties, who I later learned was a Jew. I introduced myself and told him about Kolka's plan. Klim told me not to worry: we would meet in Jedlanka the next day and sort things out.

I had just finished talking to the major when a man with a short beard approached. He looked like a Jew, and I invited him to come along with us when we went back to the village to ask for shelter. He turned out to be a Jewish poet and satirist from Warsaw named Stanislaw Jerzy Lec. He spent the night with us but later went his own way, and became one of postwar Poland's most famous writers. The peasants gave us something to eat and prepared our beds. In the morning, they gave us breakfast and a glass of vodka. Afterward, I said that I was going to go looking for Kolka.

I left my submachine gun and ammunition belt on my bed. I took off my holsters and left them there as well. The only weapon I took was my Luger, which I had taken from the German gendarme that I had killed. I got on my bike and rode until I saw Kolka walking toward me. I got off my bike and said, "You asked me to come. Here I am."

He gave me an angry look. "You Jews have machine guns and sit around all day doing nothing," he said.

"You have nothing to say to me, you piece of shit," I said. "You're not my commander."

There were several hundred AL partisans garrisoned in the village, and many of them were just hanging around. He ordered two of them to arrest me. They took my bicycle, but they did not search me. When Kolka asked me where my men were, I refused to tell him. But a farmer who knew me innocently told him which house my men were staying in.

When we got to the front of the house, which had a little fence with a gate before it, Finkel and Felusz were sitting on the stoop, polishing their boots. The moment I opened the gate, I pushed the two men who had arrested me aside and yelled, "Sam, Felusz, don't give them our guns!" They ran into the house and grabbed their submachine guns. I followed and grabbed mine. At that point, Kolka, waving his pistol wildly, burst into the house.

"If you want our guns, you can have them over our dead bodies," I said.

He turned to Felusz, who was a gentile, and asked him why he was mixed up with us.

"He is now my commander," Felusz replied.

Suddenly, hundreds of partisans, villagers, and farmers gathered in front of the house. Two AL party members in civilian clothes walked in and escorted Kolka out of the house. Later, one of them came back in and told me that I was to return to my area and stay there pending the arrival in Bojki of Chief of Staff Volinski.

A week later, I got a message from AL headquarters that Volinski had arrived, so I took my group of fifteen men with me to Bojki. I reported to Volinski, who was surrounded by ten men seated at a table. He told me, laughing, that Kolka had filed charges against me. He asked me why I hadn't shot the son of a bitch, told me not to worry, and said that he knew the whole story—there had been plenty of witnesses.

The next day, Kolka saw me on the street and saluted me as if nothing had happened. Later, after the war, he tried to make a joke out of the incident. After he and Chiel, Dworecki, and I had had a few drinks, he said, "That son of a bitch, Skinny Frank, wouldn't let himself be disarmed." We never saw each other again.

While we were stationed in the village of Bojki, we learned that several partisans from General Baranowski's group, the ATRAT, had captured two spies in Ostrow-Lubelski. The partisans brought them to the forest nearby and were preparing to execute them when Sam Gruber and Mikolai Berezin arrived, just in time: they recognized the "spies" as Joseph Cynowiec and his girlfriend, Irka. She had been living in an apartment in the Lublin area on Aryan papers and had hidden Joseph there. Upon their release, they became part of our group. After the war, Joseph went to Israel and became an officer in the Israeli Army. He married Irka and, strange as it may seem, they established a pig farm in Israel.

On May 20, all the fighters who had taken part in the battle in Rablow dispersed as planned. Most of us, including my platoon, went back to Parczew Forest, where we had cover and could set up defensive positions and make camp. The forest was our home base, which we would leave when the Germans threatened to destroy us and return to when they had pulled out. Unfortunately, on the way back to the forest, Brigadier Commander Skotnicki was killed—a blow to us and to the AL, because he was a great leader. He was posthumously awarded the rank of major and given the Gruenwald Cross, and his remains were buried with those of the Polish national war heroes in the military cemetery at Warsaw.

On returning to Parczew Forest, we joined up with the rest of Chiel Grynszpan's group in the village of Kodeniec, where he had established headquarters. There we learned that the military situation in the area had changed, with many partisan units having crossed from the east of the Bug River to the west, in anticipation of the Russian offensive. We also learned that Chiel's group had narrowly escaped being ambushed in the village of Wola Wereszczynska. My future brother-in-law Abie, who was all of ten years old, was riding through the village on horseback when he noticed Germans sneaking through the fields. He warned Chiel's men, and they were able to ambush the Germans, who had to pull back.

In Kodeniec, Dworecki, Peltz, and I shared lodgings with a farmer, and we all got along well, although we had different personalities. Peltz was a show-off and a braggart. Dworecki—intelligent and courageous—was a really good friend, despite the ten-year difference in our ages.

Several women were full members of our groups; they helped out by cooking and washing for the men. Chiel's group included Roska Duman, Tema, Pesel, and Cesia Pomeranc, who, with her brothers and parents, had been a slave laborer before escaping to the forest. Sam Gruber felt sorry for Cesia because he saw that the older women were giving her the least pleasant chores to do. He sent her over to talk to me. He thought maybe she could help out with the cooking for Dworecki, Peltz, and me.

Cesia brought her ten-year-old brother, Abie, along with her to the farmhouse. It was a log house, with small stone steps in front and a well between the house and the barn. It was something out of a folktale. I was struck by her appearance. She was shy and exotically beautiful. She was eighteen years old. Abie, too shy to meet me, ran outside and watched us through the window, standing on a block. Cesia told me that she was from the village of Wyryki near the river town of Wlodowa and that two of her brothers—Jurek and Janek—were fighting with the partisans. They were the only other survivors from a family of nine. Janek had been heavily wounded; she described to me how she had helped save him, bandaging his wounds and helping to carry him to a farmer, begging for food and medicines. Later, he was taken by Russian partisans across the Bug River. She had no idea where he was or if he was still alive. As she spoke, I thought of my own sisters. It struck me that she could have been one of them. I decided right there and then to help and shelter her.

Cesia's Story

I was born on March 15, 1926, in Wyryki, just west of Wlodowa, a Polish city on the Bug River. By the time the Germans invaded Poland, we were a family of nine. I had three brothers—Jurek, Janek, and Abie—and three sisters: Chaia, Matele, and Chanele. I was the third oldest. My mother's parents lived with us until they passed away; that was before the Germans came. We had a nice, single-family house with about two acres of land, with a little orchard of apple and plum and pear trees. We had no running water in the house, but there was a well in the backyard. In general, we had a good life. We had domestic help twice a week, and we always had enough food to eat.

In our free time, after school and on weekends, Chaia and I helped my mother take care of our younger sisters and do the housekeeping. We attended the public school and had a tutor from the Wlodowa Yeshiva for Jewish studies and prayer. We celebrated all the Jewish holidays. Around Passover and the New Year we bought new shoes and clothes. In 1939, my sister Chaia left with her fiancé for the Russian side of the Bug. We never saw her again.

My mother, Bella Ita, whose maiden name was Glincman,

was a good wife, a good mother, a wonderful, warmhearted woman. She was a talented cook, always preparing delicious meals for the family and our frequent guests. My father, Lazar Pomeranc, was in the lumber business. He would hire an estimator to choose mature trees in forests owned by churches and estates and to calculate how much timber he could get out of each tree. After the trees were felled and the limbs lopped, the logs were loaded onto rafts and transported over the waterways to lumber companies in the area. It was a thriving business.

The German occupation brought terror to our home. Whenever we heard rumors that the Germans were coming through our village, it was my job to take my two little sisters up to the attic and hide with them there until the Germans left the house. I would stand with them, sometimes for hours, and when I heard the sound of boot steps I would cover their mouths with my hands so that they could not make a sound and give us away.

One evening, all nine of us were sitting at the dinner table when suddenly two German officers appeared at the door. One of them came in, and when he saw our family sitting all together, he said to my father, "Take them to the Russian side. Here they will all be killed." My parents were shocked. We had not heard that Jews were being systematically killed or even deported. My father thought about Kaiser Wilhelm and the German Army in World War I; the Germans had not been particularly anti-Semitic. He had an ingrained distrust of the Russians and assumed that, under the Germans, life would go on pretty much as before. He never imagined that we would be killed just for being Jews. In any case, how could we just pick up and go, with such a large family? We knew no one on the other side of the Bug. How could our parents feed us? At least at home we knew farmers and other Poles who could help us obtain food.

In 1942, when I was sixteen, the Germans deported my entire family from Wyryki to work as slave laborers at a labor camp in Adampol, a nearby estate owned by Count Zamoyski. My father was assigned to work at the stables with the camp horses. My mother and all the children, except for my little brother Abie, worked in the fields, harvesting fruit and potatoes. The head of the camp, a man named Salinger, became very fond of Abie and always took him with him. Abie became Salinger's little pet, and Salinger let him ride the horses and indulged him with treats.

We had worked at Adampol for a few months when rumors began to spread around the camp that the Germans were rounding up Jews in the surrounding towns and villages and sending them away. We also heard that people, mostly teen-agers and those in their twenties, had run away before the roundups and were hiding in the woods. My father became convinced that we could escape, for though there were plenty of German gendarmes keeping a watchful eye on us, the estate was not very well secured. My cousins Jurek and Mordecai Cholomsky, along with their father, Avram, were among those who had fled from their town into the woods, and a few days later Jurek, who knew we had been taken to Adampol, made up his mind to try to rescue us.

When Jurek showed up at Adampol, I tried to conceal my emotions on seeing him. I remember that he had a gun, which he hid in one of the stables. The Germans must have noticed this new face or have been tipped off, because later that day, they came to search the stable and found the gun. The next thing I knew, they were leading Jurek and my brother Janek away to the bank of a ravine, where they had rounded up more than eighty people. One of the German gendarmes came up to Jurek and looked deeply into his face as he spoke to him. "You're a good-looking boy. You have beautiful eyes. I have a son about your age. He's in the German Army and he looks so much like you. It's really too bad that I have to kill you."

Jurek whispered to Janek in Yiddish, "Whatever I do, you do it too," and he started running away from the group and toward the ravine, jumping straight down over the edge. Janek was right behind him. Shots rang out and one bullet hit Jurek in the arm, but the two kept on running toward the woods, and as they ran deeper into the forest, with the trees protecting them, they were saved. Janek tore off a piece of his shirt and wrapped it around Jurek's arm to stop the bleeding, and after several hours, they made it back to the campsite.

We learned about this only later, but the next day, my father decided that my oldest brother, whose name was also Jurek, should try to steal out of Adampol late that night and go into the forest and look for my brother and cousin and report back. When Jurek returned, he told us that he had seen little children and women living at a campsite. Some were from our town. So my father decided that my brother Jurek and I should go into the forest and join the others.

"You go, the two of you," he said, "and we will come in two days, because I want to get some handguns so we can defend ourselves before we go."

He had been working alongside some Polish gentiles and thought that he would be able to get at least one or two revolvers from them. Later that night, Jurek and I stole out of Adampol for the campsite in the woods, and there we were reunited with our brother Janek and our cousins. The boys set about finding a hiding place for me in the root cellar of a Polish farmhouse. I was there for only one night—a night of pure terror. When they returned the next day with food, I told them that I could not remain alone in the cellar. "Can you imagine what would happen to me if the Germans were to find me? What they might do to me?" I insisted on remaining with them, even if it meant dying with them.

Several days later, we heard that the Germans had taken ten Jewish families to the edge of a ditch in Adampol and shot them all. A few days later, a Polish farmer came to our campsite in the woods with a dirty little boy, asking if anyone recognized him. I looked up and said, "This is my little brother." It was Abie, who was ten years old. Years later, we pieced together the story from eyewitnesses. After executing the families, including my beloved parents and sisters, the Germans checked to make sure that everyone was dead, and left. But Abie was small, and somehow the bullets missed him. He fell into the pit with the family, unwounded, and lay there. Later that day, he crawled out of the pit and ran into the forest by himself, looking for us, when the Polish farmer found him, crying and filthy.

After a while, Janek went with Jurek into a village to get bread, and somewhere between the woods and the village a Ukrainian shot Janek. Jurek grabbed Janek and brought him to the woods. Janek had been shot in the side and the bullet had gone out his back. When I saw how much blood he was losing, I ripped apart a linen shirt and put some threads in the bullet hole to serve as a dressing. He was conscious but looked as if he was dying. I left Jurek to watch Janek, and I took Abie so that I wouldn't be alone. Together, we went into Wyryki to the home of a man we knew and who liked us very much. I knocked on the door in the night and said, "Listen, they have shot Janek and we do not have anything. We have no bread." He said, "Shhh, be quiet." He gave us two loaves of bread and some little tablets, like aspirin, and a bottle of milk. "Come," he said, "I'll take you out so nobody will see you."

When we got back to Janek, I gave him the pills to ease the pain. We sat with him for two days, and then Jurek and I carried him through the forest until we found the camp. The partisans tried to help Janek, but he was very sick. Then some Russian partisans arrived and suggested that they take him across the Bug River to a partisan camp where there were Russian doctors. We let him go with them, and I did not see Janek again for two years. He spent all that time with the Voroshilov partisan group.

One day, some Polish people alerted us that Germans were in the area. Many of our men were off fighting, and we were just sitting around when suddenly we heard someone say in German through a megaphone, "Everybody come out." We thought, It's all over. Our lives are finished. It wouldn't be easy to run away because we had children and older people with us. The Germans hadn't yet seen us. They were just calling into the forest, "Come out! We won't shoot." We all began to walk toward the edge of the forest in the direction of a great meadow. My brother Jurek told me to take Abie and go back into the forest. We took his advice and crawled back on our stomachs. Jurek had seen the Germans. Then we got up and began to run. Two young German soldiers, about our age, saw us, but they did nothing. They let us go. Who knows why they let us go?

When we got back into the forest, we sat and listened. Suddenly, we heard shooting, shooting, shooting. Then it stopped and everything was quiet. Jurek, Abie, and I, and Szaia Pomeranc, who was not a relative, and two men from Wlodowa were safe. All the others—classmates, townspeople, women and children—had been killed.

We moved around for several weeks with my cousin Jurek Cholomsky, who had shown great courage in coming to Adampol to warn us that we would all be killed if we didn't quickly leave. My brothers and I owed our lives to him. Jurek Cholomsky's brother, Mordechai; their father, Avram; and Lonka Pfefferkorn were also part of our little group. My job was to help with the cooking for the entire group. Later, Jurek Cholomsky, who was a very courageous fighter, joined up with Chiel Grynszpan near Ochoza. Grynszpan was the leader of ninety-five fighting men. The two men took an immediate liking to each other, and Chiel had complete confidence in my cousin. As we moved around, we took in other Jews who were in the forests struggling to survive. Finally, there were about a hundred and twenty-five of us. The Germans were constantly hunting for us.

Grynszpan's group joined forces with the group of Sam Gruber, Marion Dworecki, and Franek Blajchman. One day, we were quartered in Kodeniec. Chiel Grynszpan and Sam Gruber were quartered in one house; Marion, Franek, and Franek's assistant, Moishe Peltz, were in another.

Chiel introduced me to Sam Gruber, and it was through Sam that I met Franek. I found Sam to be a very nice person with a pleasant smile. Often, while passing by where we cooked, he would stop to chat with us and ask one or two of us where we were from. He noticed that the older women were pushing me around, giving me the least pleasant tasks. I saw that this disturbed him.

About two weeks after this, Sam asked me to come outside and talk with him. He asked if I would like to change my circumstances. He said that he could refer me to his friend Franek, whom he had known for a year and a half, and said he was a good man. I could have an easier job. He had told Franek about me, and Franek had agreed to interview me for a job helping out with the cooking.

I took my younger brother Abie and went to meet him. When I arrived, Franek greeted me at the door and introduced me to Dworecki and Peltz, his two housemates. Abie was very shy. He ran outside and watched us through the window. Franek asked where I came from. I told him and explained that my family had been murdered by the Nazis and that I had two surviving brothers who were with me, Abie and Jurek, and that my third brother, Janek, had been wounded and taken across the Bug River, and we did not know if he was alive.

Franek said that he remembered having met Jurek several months before, in March, with the Wanda Waszylewska partisan group in a forest east of the Bug and that they had returned to this side together.

We talked for about fifteen minutes. I liked the way Franek looked at me. He said that there were just the three of them to cook for and that I was welcome to try it out and free to go at any time if I felt uncomfortable. I decided to see how things went. After several days, I realized that I liked the way Franek and the others behaved toward me. He treated me like a sister. So I stayed with them.

As if Cesia needed to prove something, or maybe to express her gratitude for our willingness to accept her, she asked the farmer's wife for flour, eggs, cheese, and other ingredients and set about making pierogi and blintzes for us. Once I tasted her cooking, I knew that I had made the right decision; she cooked the same way my mother had. I gave her a big compliment—and she stayed. The farmer's wife offered Cesia the extra bed in the house. After lunch, Dworecki and I sat for a while talking about our unit and Cesia went over to her bed to sit. When I noticed Peltz sitting beside her and flirting, I gave him a fierce look and said three words in Yiddish: *"Rik seich aveck!"* ("Move yourself away.")

He did—and never tried to flirt with her again. Nobody around her dared to touch her or speak rudely to her, including me. During the many months I spent in the forest, I treated other women with similar respect, never expecting favors in return. All I had to do was imagine what my sisters would be going through in their place.

Early one morning while we were stationed in Kodeniec, Jurek, Cesia's older brother, brought a young Polish boy to me. He said that he was eighteen years old and wanted to become a partisan. Jurek, always alert, had been quick to sense that this boy wasn't telling the truth. After exchanging a few words with him, I, too, smelled a rat. The boy was carrying a box of yarn and said that he was a peddler who had recently been drafted into the Junak, an organization that supplied young Poles to work as slave laborers for Germany, and that he had escaped.

I was too busy with Dworecki to speak with the boy at any length at that moment, so I invited him to hang around with the group for a while. Then, if he still wanted to join us, he could come back after lunch and we could admit him. I told Jurek to keep an eye on the boy and, if he tried to leave the village, grab him and bring him back to me. About fifteen minutes later, Jurek returned, pushing the fellow by the scruff of his neck. The boy had tried to slip away.

Sam Gruber and I started interrogating him. The first question I asked him was why he would want to join an all-Jewish group when there were plenty of gentile partisan units in the area. Sam was sitting there, with a pad and pencil, taking down his replies. When the boy refused to talk, I applied a little stick on his elbows and ankles to make him reconsider. It turned out that he wasn't as young as he looked: he was in his twenties and a German agent whose mission was to make contact with partisan groups and find out how many there were, how well armed, and what their plans were. He named three of his contacts in different villages. Now that our groups were reunited and under Chiel's command, I felt free to use men from his group. This was Chiel's territory, and his men knew their way around it better than anyone else, so we sent some of them to pick up the three contacts. Chiel's men captured them and brought them in for questioning. Two of them admitted to collaborating with the Germans, each for the same reason: because he had family members who had been taken to concentration camps. When the Germans promised that the relatives would be released if they collaborated, the men agreed. The third man persisted in claiming that he was innocent.

I had a hunch that something was wrong here. I went back to the spy, who laughed and said, "Until you beat me up, I didn't admit to anything either." So once again we interrogated the third man, using force, until we realized that he would never admit to being a collaborator. So now we went back to the spy and worked him over until, finally, he admitted that the third man was, in fact, innocent. Totally confused, I asked why he had claimed that the man was guilty. It turned out that the third man had once insulted his mother; the spy was using us to take his revenge!

The author's family. Top, left to right: Chaim Israel Blajchman (father); Brocha Blajchman Cohen (cousin); Ita Lewin Blajchman (mother); Revan Cohen (cousin); Esther Blajchman Cohen (aunt); Uncle Moishe's daughter, Esther Blajchman (cousin); Josef Blajchman (uncle); Faiga Blajchman (cousin). Middle row: Grandfather Beryl Blajchman; Grandmother Chana Gittle Blajchman; Aunt Dvora Blajchman Weislater. Bottom row: Sister Sara; the author; unknown child; cousin Rose Blajchman; two unknown children.

Grandfather Beryl Blajchman and Grandmother Chana Gittle Blajchman. All the family photos were taken in the 1930s. The few on these pages are the only ones that survived the Holocaust.

Sara Blajchman, the author's sister.

Escape from Kamionka: Count Zamoyski's palace in Kozlowka (above), where the author spent the first night of his flight from Kamionka in a room off the kitchen. Two Jewish boys he knew were working as slave laborers there. From the palace he made his way to the Klos family farm and from there to Bratnik Forest, where many Jews were hiding in bunkers.

Sever Rubinstein (left), his sister Blimka, and Michael Loterstein. These photos were taken in 1944.

The author, left, and Sam Finkel.

Marion Dworecki in Polish officer's uniform, 1944.

Left to right: The author, Francziszek Volinski (with field glasses), Jan Wojtovitcz, and Pawel Dubek, AL staff officers.

Members of Chiel Grynszpan's group. Left to right, standing: David Rubinstein, Jurek Pomeranc, Lonka Pfefferkorn, Lova Zicman, Chiel Grynszpan, Welve Litwak, Joseph Rolnik, an unidentified Russian soldier. Kneeling: Abraham Rubinstein, Henry Barbanel, Kirlow Rubinstein. Later, when the Polish Armia Ludowa, or AL, took command of the Jewish partisan units, Grynszpan was appointed commander of the Jewish group, Sam Gruber was second in command, and Marion Dworecki and the author were platoon commanders.

Other members of Grynszpan's group. Left to right, standing: Harold Werner, Sam Barbanel, Dora and Abram Grynszpan (wife and husband), and Velvale Patsan. Kneeling: Shienka, Abraham Rubinstein, and Henry Barbanel.

The author's cousin Froim Lewin, a young man at the time, escaped from Warsaw, bringing his little brother Usher with him. Froim was a member of the twelve-man defense unit formed in Bratnik Forest at the author's urging. He became a dedicated and courageous fighter.

The author, left, and Sam Gruber, following their appointment by the AL as platoon commanders with the rank of second lieutenant.

Cesia Pomeranc was one of a family of nine that escaped being massacred by the Nazis. She and three of her brothers found refuge in Parczew Forest, where they became part of Chiel Grynszpan's group.

Jurek Cholomsky, a cousin of Cesia Pomeranc, risked his life to warn the Pomeranc family that they would be killed if they did not leave Adampol quickly. His action saved many lives. He later became a member of Chiel Grynszpan's group. Brigadier Commander Alexander Skotnicki, who led a united partisan force of 1,300, chose Jurek as his aide and guide when the Germans tried to surround and destroy the partisans in Parczew Forest prior to the Soviet offensive.

Cesia Pomeranc's mother, Bella Ita, with daughter Chaia.

Cesia's father, Lazar Pomeranc, in a portrait based on the memory of his son Janek.

Cesia Pomeranc with other members of Chiel Grynszpan's partisan group.

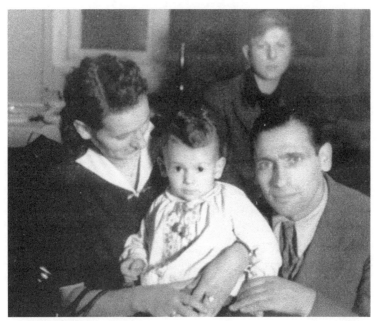

Dobay and Berek Tunkelschwartz with their daughter Brenda.

The author was promoted to first lieutenant and awarded the Cross of Valor.

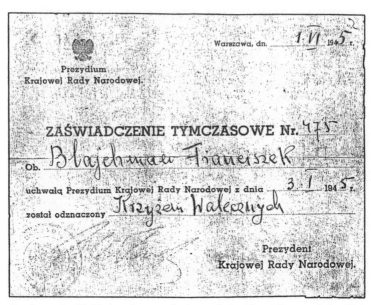

On June 1, 1945, by the resolution of the Presidium of the Polish National Council, the author was decorated with the Cross of Valor.

Two weeks after being awarded the Cross of Valor, the author was promoted to the rank of first lieutenant, "for meritorious service in the partisan struggle" in an order signed by General Michael Rola-Zymierski, supreme commander of the Polish Army.

Cesia Pomeranc and Frank at their wedding in Lubartow, Poland, on September 6, 1945.

Left to right: Janek, Avram, and Jurek Pomeranc, with Cesia Pomeranc-Blaichman and the author after the wedding.

Left to right: Berek Tunkelschwartz, Cesia, Dobay Tunkelschwartz, the author, and Marion Dworecki.

Aron and
Regina Gotz.

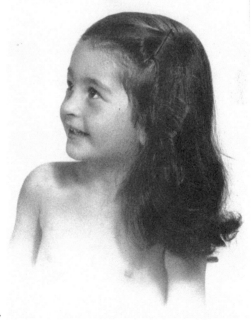

Bella.

Monument to the massacre at Adampol that makes no mention of Jews, even though all the people murdered were Jews.

The author delivering his "Address at the Unveiling of the Jewish Fighters Monument" at Yad Vashem, Jerusalem, May 6, 1985.

We consulted with the AL's intelligence group. It confirmed that the first two men had been coerced into becoming
collaborators, but that the third one, who had a good name
in his village, was innocent. Under these circumstances, the
final decision was to let all three men go with a warning that,
if there was a next time, they would be shot. As for the spy, we
executed him and later learned that he was the man who had
provided the Germans with the location of Chiel Grynszpan's
camp at Wola Wereszczynska.

At the end of May 1944, there was a change of the AL's
command in the Lublin district. Commander Moczar was
transferred to the Kielce district, near Radom. He had always
been supportive of all the Jewish partisan groups, supplying
us with arms and sufficient backup for dangerous operations.
He never singled out Jews for especially dangerous missions, a
tactic favored by anti-Semitic Communist commanders. In his
place, the AL appointed Ignacy Robb Narbut, who was soon
replaced by Grzegorz Korcinzki, formerly an AL commander
the Janov Forest. He was one of those responsible for sending
Jewish fighters into a suicidal battle against German tanks.

In early June, we met in the village of Przpisowka with
Wojtovitcz, Volinski, Marzenta, and Kolka, and learned that
on June 6, Stalin had received General Rola-Zymierski, the
head of all AL forces in Poland, in Moscow to discuss the
offensive. At their meeting, Stalin made a commitment to
send enough munitions and equipment to arm an additional
two hundred thousand men.

CHAPTER VI

FINAL ENGAGEMENTS AND THE GERMAN RETREAT

FROM JUNE 15 THROUGH JULY 10, 1944, several airdrops of arms and men increased the fighting power of the partisans. At the end of the month, the AL ordered us to secure the area for a parachute drop in Parczew Forest. That night, the Russians parachuted in more than a hundred well-equipped soldiers under the command of a Captain Trucker. They wore the uniforms of the Polish Army, but many of them did not speak Polish. These troops included intelligence officers under the command of the local AL, which deployed them westward toward the Vistula River. As the troops spread through the countryside, Polish villagers, astonished to see them, hugged and kissed them as liberators.

By the beginning of July, the entire Parczew Forest area

had become a giant partisan camp. We destroyed several German trains heavily loaded with supplies, on their way to the front, including some on the Radzyn-Lublin line and one German troop train on the Parczew-Lublin line. As a result, the Germans mobilized a large force to rid the area of partisans. They brought in three Waffen SS battalions from Lublin, Bialystok, and Pulawy under SS Commander Lippmann, four gendarmerie battalions in armored personnel carriers, and one cavalry battalion.

All partisan groups in the area continued to move into Parczew Forest. These included Chiel's group, to which we belonged; Korcinzki's men; the AL; the AK's Twenty-seventh Division; Baranowski's men; Czerny's group; the Bielowa group; Roskowski's group; and Janowski's group—all told, more than ten thousand men. Each group was assigned to a specific area and took up defensive positions, digging trenches and setting up machine-gun emplacements. The top commanders for each group formed a central command in the middle of the forest, and all the information gathered around the forest was brought by runners to the command post.

We noticed that German troops were digging themselves in on the forest perimeter, but that their artillery was aimed eastward, toward the oncoming Russians. After several days, headquarters decided that, because we were running short on food and water and it was too dangerous to be surrounded by the German Army, all units should break out from the forest, separately and at different times.

The first to break out was the four-thousand-man-strong,

heavily armed AK. It moved out to the west in two groups. The first group met strong resistance, and both Germans and Poles took heavy casualties. The second group, which followed two hours later, encountered no resistance.

The next day, two Russian groups—Baranowski's and Czerny's—moved out to the north, without encountering German opposition. The two AL groups twice tried to break through on the south but were unsuccessful. The third time they finally made it.

On July 22, Roskowski's group tried to break through to Adampol and Zahajki and met stiff resistance. Janowski's group was right behind Roskowski's, and when the men saw what was happening, they spread out and found a break in the lines and attacked the Germans from the sides. They also radioed the Russians, who sent fighter planes to help them out. They were advised that reinforcements would be coming from Bialystok.

At this point, Chiel, Gruber, Dworecki, and I decided that it was time for our group to move out. It was a moonlit night, and I was riding on horseback toward the edge of the forest. When the woods thinned out, I noticed that the moon was reflecting off my raincoat, so I dismounted and buried the coat under a pile of leaves. We then determined where the Germans were entrenched by opening fire with one of our submachine guns. They responded with wild shooting in the air, keeping their heads down and never aiming at us, but they were easy to spot because they were using tracer bullets. Their location was roughly two hundred yards from the edge of the forest to our right. Once we had them in our sights, we took them out with mortars and hand grenades personally delivered by three of our men. We pulled out quickly without losing even one of our 120 men.

After two hours of walking, we stopped to rest at a village with a windmill at its edge and posted lookouts on the top of the mill. Exhausted, hungry, and thirsty, we asked the villagers for food and shelter, and they provided both. I was thinking of shaving and asked Cesia for my knapsack. She was responsible for carrying it; in addition to my shaving equipment, it always contained a fresh change of underwear and a clean shirt. Cesia looked around and realized that, while crawling and running for her life through the forest, she must have dropped the knapsack. At the time, I was very annoyed. It was only later that I was able to laugh at myself for losing my temper over such a little thing.

At around 10:00 a.m., our lookouts on top of the windmill reported seeing four Germans on horseback approaching the village. We woke everyone up and told them to go into the fields where there was good cover and to trench in and take up defensive positions.

An hour later, we heard a low rumble, like thunder. The ground began to tremble. Through my binoculars I saw a column of German tanks coming straight toward us from the village. I was dug in alongside Gruber, Chiel, and Dworecki. We told our men to be ready, but not to open fire until ordered. I saw the column turn left onto a field road that ran parallel to our position; the Germans were now only about a hundred yards from us. We became alarmed because it looked as though they were on their way to engage us in battle. With our weapons and numbers, we could not possibly engage a column of tanks. My mind was racing: how could we escape? We sent out scouts behind our positions to find a way out. I looked through my binoculars again and saw that the Germans were not combat-ready; instead, they were sitting on top of their tanks. At this moment, our scouts returned to report that all the roads behind us were filled with German trucks, tanks, and horse-drawn wagons moving west. They weren't coming after us; they were trying to get away from the Russian Army as fast as they could. What I was looking at was the Nazi war machine in retreat.

We could not move. There was nowhere to go. Hiding in the fields, trenched in, we heard the decisive battles for our area. The forest was full of Russian partisans. When they saw the Germans moving out on all the roads, they called on their air force to bomb and strafe the columns. When the Germans tried to take cover in the forest, the partisans cut them down with their heavy machine guns. Then the Germans called in the Luftwaffe, and we watched the dogfights above the forest off to the east.

It took hours for the tank columns to pass our positions. Our men later said that some of the Germans riding on the tanks must have spotted us, but just looked the other way. To this day, I can't imagine how we managed to keep cool in a situation like this, when we could all have been killed and our only defense was in lying low and waiting it out. We had become a tightly disciplined group. Nobody made a false move.

About half an hour after the last tank passed, we heard a

huge explosion and saw flames and smoke maybe a thousand feet behind us. We later learned that one of the German tanks had broken down; the Germans blew it up, not wanting to leave it behind for the Russians.

When night fell, the roads were still crowded with thousands upon thousands of German foot soldiers riding on trucks, wagons, and horses. It was this congestion that had forced the tanks to take to the smaller roads through fields and forests. We had not eaten since the previous day. The tension was wearing on us. We began to move out from our positions through the high grasses and swamps on the margins of a meadow, trying to find a break in the German encirclement. But after we had crossed the meadow, we came to another road, also crowded with Germans. I sent a man out to scout for yet another way through the German lines. Kneeling there on one knee, resting my elbow against the disk of my submachine gun, I dozed off. When I woke up, everyone was gone. I whistled our signal, and a German flare burst over my head. When the flare died out, I started running for my life. At the same moment, the heavens opened and the rain came down in stinging, driving sheets. It was a tremendous downpour. Through the sheets of rain, I could see horses, cows, and figures moving in the distance, and I headed toward them, with my submachine gun at the ready. Coming closer, I saw some farmers sitting around a roofed haystack with blankets over their heads. I asked if they had seen any partisans come by. They told me that a group had gone by just a few minutes before.

Then one of them asked, *"Amchu?"*

"*Amchu,*" I replied.

He told me his name. I recognized it and told him that his son was our guide.

The sky was starting to lighten on a new day. I dug a hole in a haystack and asked the man to cover me up, and soon I fell into a deep sleep. Later that morning, I crawled out of the haystack and was relieved to find that my now-rusted submachine gun was still working. Looking around, I saw horses and cows wandering in the pasture. This struck me as strange, because normally they would be in their stalls behind the farmers' houses in the village. What was going on? I wondered, and then understood that everyone had evacuated the village to be out of the way when the Germans moved through.

The farmers had covered the horses and cows with patchwork blankets made out of old clothes, to keep them from getting chilled. I looked down at what I was wearing: my officer's uniform with its belt and pistol at my side, bandolier across my chest, grenades and submachine gun. It all made me a walking target for the Germans. I pulled a blanket off one of the cows, wrapped it around myself, and walked on. Eventually, I saw a peasant approaching and asked him if he would buy some food for me, and I offered him money. He said that he didn't want any money but that he would be glad to bring me some food. A few minutes later, he brought bread and butter, farmer's cheese, and some milk. He also brought news. He said he had heard that the Russian Army was only a few kilometers away.

As I sat down to eat, artillery shells began exploding, creating craters in the rain-soaked ground all around me. I assumed it was Russian artillery, as I knew that the Germans were running like rats. One shell landed so close by that it splashed mud all over me. I ran over to one of the first craters, figuring that by this time the artillerymen would have adjusted their range. I was cold, wet, dirty, tired, and wondering about my chances of survival when I saw in the distance some men scrambling up from where they had taken shelter and recognized them as my own. They excitedly told me they had heard that the Russian Army was in the village of Kuninka, about five kilometers away.

On the way to Kuninka, some of our men stopped in one of the villages to get food and saw forty or more German stragglers, their rifles down by their side, probably also looking for food. When my men opened fire, the Germans ran for their lives. We didn't bother chasing them down, but took some food and went on slogging through the fields, eager to make contact with the Russians.

Shortly after noon, just outside Kuninka, I saw something moving in the distance and, using binoculars, spotted camouflaged tanks. They were approaching us on a road that made a wide curve around the meadow we were in. I was still trying to figure out whose tanks they were when I saw a figure on horseback riding toward us through the meadow. I could tell he was a Russian officer by the red band around his hat. When he greeted us in Russian I knew that the worst was over. We had survived.

It was about noon when the Red Army colonel led us into the village. The Russians must have arrived a few hours before, but the peasants and the soldiers and officers were still hugging one another and kissing in the streets. It was like a huge family reunion, everyone coming together after not having seen each other for years. People were laughing and crying, with relief, with happiness, and we were crying too. The people had opened their doors to the Russians and now they opened their doors to us and welcomed us in and put everything they had to eat and drink on the table. They may have thought we were Poles because our commanders, myself included, were wearing Polish officer uniforms. Maybe the people of Kuninka would have welcomed us just as heartily if they had known we were Jews. It was a day for rejoicing.

We drank and we stuffed ourselves with eggs and cheese and butter and milk and honey and meat and we sang—Russians and Poles, gentiles and Jews. One of the Russians had a balalaika and we sang Russian songs, and our Jewish partisan group sang along with him. I still remember those songs, very flowery and romantic, about beautiful women. And then there was the song about the mother who loses a son who has gone to fight with the partisans, and she laments that her son's wife will find another husband but she herself will not find another son. There was another song we sang—the song of a fighter in a bunker who knows that death is only a few yards away, while home is far away and the road is rough and rugged.

So we sang and Cesia was rejoicing there with her brothers Jurek and Abie. We all drank *Bimber*—Polish homemade vodka—for hours, until many of us, myself included, were good and drunk.

The next morning, we sobered up, and the realization that we had in fact survived overwhelmed us. We thought of our fallen comrades, who did not have the chance to see this day of liberation. Most of all, we thought of our families and loved ones. None of us knew exactly what had happened to them. Some of my comrades had seen their families murdered before their eyes; the rest of us were holding on to the hope that at least some members of our family might still be alive.

The brutal murder of our families could have made us lose our humanity, but it had not. We were proud that, although we were a terrorized group of young people who had been turned into orphans overnight, we had not lowered ourselves to the level of the enemy but, while we had killed those we found guilty, had done everything in our power to avoid harming innocent people.

THAT SAME DAY, the AL notified us that we—the Jewish partisans and the Polish partisans—were now officially part of the Polish government. Grynszpan-Gruber's group was assigned to Lublin; Dworecki and I were transferred to Lubartow and assigned to the Polish Security Police. We asked our officers if we could have some time off to start our search for any family members who may have survived. They granted us leave and told us to report to them when we were done.

Dworecki, Finkel, Rubinstein, Eisenberg, and my cousin Froim and I hitched a ride to Kamionka in a Russian Army truck. A procession was just coming out of the Catholic church as we arrived. The parishioners were carrying statues of Jesus and Mary down the middle of the main street in front of the town hall. We were standing on one side of the square, the same square in which I had stood in September 1939, when our mayor announced that the war had begun, and where, only a few weeks later, I had watched Germans beating up Hasidim. Two men who recognized us left the procession and came over. "Thank you for killing our brother," one of them said sarcastically. I remembered that we had executed him for collaborating with the Germans, as well as for killing Jews who had been in hiding. Finkel lifted his submachine gun, but I grabbed at the magazine and yanked it out just in time to prevent him from doing anything foolish. The two men ran behind the town hall and off into the meadows that used to be my playground and where so many of our people had been executed.

The Twenty-seventh Division of the AK was stationed in and around Kamionka. Perhaps these two guys thought that they could say such things with impunity and that the AK would take its revenge on us. About a hundred feet away, we noticed several AK officers, wearing Polish uniforms and talking to the mayor. Normally, we would be nervous with so many AK people around, but the six of us weren't afraid. An endless stream of Russian troops was moving through the town, on foot and in trucks and tanks. We could count on their protection.

I called the mayor over and asked him to arrange for transportation for us; it was my way of demonstrating our lack of fear. He said that he would take care of this for us—on the double.

We walked over to a restaurant and ordered lunch, and, after thinking it over, decided we would be better off hitching a ride out of town with Russians, even though the mayor had already arranged a carriage and driver for us. We figured we would be vulnerable to an ambush by the AK men or any other bunch of punks. We jumped onto the Russian tanks heading toward Michow and spent eight days in the area, asking a lot of questions about our families, and never getting an answer.

Dworecki and I said goodbye to our friends and headed back to Lubartow, while the others went to their assignments in Lublin. Our police commander arranged for us to share a pleasant two-bedroom apartment in a two-story building in the center of Lubartow that had previously been occupied by German officers—quite a change from the bunkers in the woods and the simple peasant farmhouses we had grown accustomed to. Our commander also provided us with an office in a building just across the street, and two secretaries. Dworecki and I found an abandoned BMW Nazi-issue motorcycle with a sidecar, which we shared, and since we weren't under tight control, two or three times a week we would take an afternoon ride to Lublin to see our friends and Cesia, with whom I had remained close.

For the next six months—from July 1944 until January 1945—Dworecki and I were assigned to a unit of the Polish Security Police responsible for hunting down and investigating Nazi collaborators: Poles, Ukrainians, and Volksdeutsche (the term used for people of German ancestry who had settled outside of Germany—in Poland and the Ukraine, for example).

With lists of suspects found in Nazi payroll records, some of which we had stolen in partisan raids on Nazi offices, we went from village to village, questioning people and interrogating suspects. Many villagers were no longer afraid to cooperate fully with us. The war in our area was over, the Germans defeated, and most people understood that these collaborators were now the enemies of the new Poland as well. Our assignment was not to apprehend collaborators—only to determine their whereabouts, look for witnesses, and report what we had gathered to headquarters. Our superiors then sent out agents who made the arrests. We discovered that a number of collaborators had fled west to areas still under German control; we kept that information for use when in due course they were captured. Each Friday, we prepared reports and sent them to the head of our department.

In September or October of 1944, the local newspapers reported that two former Nazi guards at Majdanek Concentration Camp had been tried and sentenced to death by hanging. We knew that when the camp was liberated in July, the Russian Army had captured many Nazi guards and officers who had run the gas chambers at the death camp. An announcement published in the papers stated the date and time that the hanging would occur outside of Zamek Prison, in Lublin, and requested that all citizens attend to witness the carrying out of the sentence. For us, the partisans—especially those of us who were Jews—the news had a tremendous emotional impact. We had lived to see the Polish government begin to bring brutal Nazi murderers to justice. Thousands of people from throughout the area came to witness the executions, which were held in the field outside the prison walls. My partisan cousin Froim, whose father, Mayer Lewin, had been gassed at Majdanek, was given the honor of placing the noose around the neck of one of the condemned guards. Overwhelmed with emotion, we wept openly.

In addition to fulfilling our assigned duties, Dworecki and I decided to see if we could track down any Jewish survivors in Lubartow. We found a family named Tunkelschwartz that had survived in hiding. Berek Tunkelschwartz was in his forties, a tall, hardworking, pious man. His wife, Dobay, was in poor health, very thin and pale; the years of terror and hiding had taken their toll on her. They had recovered their home and their oil press, used to produce flaxseed oil, which had been Berek's trade before the war. It was their livelihood. The seeds were heated and spread on the grindstone, and then Berek or his assistant would walk in a circle, pushing a wooden bar in front of him to turn the stone that pressed out the oil. It was a primitive operation, but Berek made a good living.

There were perhaps a dozen other Jews in town who had been hidden by gentiles, mostly on farms, and we all became very friendly, with the Tunkelschwartzes at the center of our social lives. One day, one of the older Jewish women we knew said something to me in Yiddish that hit home: "If you prepare yourself in your youth, you will be set in your old age." I took that to mean that we survivors should begin to marry and create families—to have children and prepare for a better future. And when I asked her, she said that was exactly what she meant.

Shortly after we arrived in Lubartow, Dworecki and I rode our motorcycle over to the Klos family farm. Once again, I received a warm welcome. The Kloses were thrilled to see me now as an officer in the Polish Army. This time, too, I felt we should not stay too long, because there were so many Jew haters in the neighborhood. The Kloses told us that they went to Lubartow every Tuesday to sell their produce at the farmers' market, and that we should stop by their stand. They would give us whatever we needed. I thanked them but assured them that we did not need anything. But each time I came to the market to see them, I took what they had brought for me—cheese, butter, honey, kielbasa, vodka—which I then gave to the Tunkelschwartzes, who so generously fed so many of us.

For as long as we were in Lubartow, we received endless invitations to dinner at their home, which we often accepted. They took pride in our armed resistance, and now that we were officers in the Polish Security Police, they felt safer when we were around.

IN JANUARY 1945, I was transferred to Kielce (Dworecki was assigned elsewhere), along with many others, and on the way there I met Sever Rubinstein. We were among the two hundred officers and one hundred security men who rode into Kielce on army trucks. We arrived at dawn and could hear the blasting of artillery about three miles to the west, where the active front was. There wasn't a soul on the streets. We got busy taking over and cleaning out three large office buildings that had been abandoned by the Germans.

At around 9:00 a.m., people started coming out of their cellars and other hiding places. Two beautiful blondes came over to our group. They seemed thrilled to see Polish officers in uniform and invited sixteen of us to breakfast—exactly the number of places at their table. The officer they spoke to picked out the guests and included Sever and me. The apartment was beautifully furnished, with an elegant dining room, and we were served like kings: eggs, cold cuts, butter, bread, sour cream, vegetables, and vodka—a real feast in those times. Sever and I looked at each other. It was clear to both of us that these two upper-class women had survived the war without enduring much hardship, which meant that they must have been Nazi and AK sympathizers. In this case, they probably did not realize who their guests were. Our Security Police uniforms camouflaged our AL connection and maybe even the fact that we were Jews. We ate, drank, said our thank-yous, and went back to work.

My job in Kielce was the same as it had been in Lubartow: to find and report the whereabouts of collaborators. This was new territory, and I had to go from village to village to question farmers and other people I had never met before. What I learned very quickly was that the whole region was infested with fascists and die-hard anti-Semites.

About a month later, I was assigned to Pinczow, where I became the assistant to the director of the Security Police. We took over a villa that had been occupied by the Germans. Two weeks later, the head of the Polish Communist Party called me into his office to ask a favor. Without knowing I was Jewish, he told me that he had a Jewish youth who had survived in hiding. The boy's name was Szymek and he was about twenty years old. The officer was afraid that local Jew haters would kill him. He asked me to give Szymek a job in the office; it could save his life.

He introduced me to the slight, redheaded boy, and the two of us went back to the villa. On the way, we chatted, and Szymek explained how well the Poles had treated him during the war. After I had listened to more buttery talk about Poles, I told him, in Yiddish, *"Schweig."* (Shut up.) And I added only one word: *"Amchu."*

His face lit up like the sun on a summer day. He never dreamed I was a Jew. I took him to the villa and told him to go take a bath. I had some extra uniforms and underwear and gave them to him. I also gave him something to eat, and while he ate, he told me how a friendly farmer had taken him in and used him to help out with farm chores. Szymek was the only member of his family to survive. He came to work at my office. To defend himself from Jew haters he might meet on the street, he made a whip out of several meters of telephone wire left behind by the Germans. Later, I gave him an automatic pistol and taught him how to use it.

Szymek was originally from a village near Pinczow, and he gave me a list of names of the Jew killers in the area. We sent investigators to the villages. Using Szymek's list, they interviewed the people he had named and found that he was telling the truth. The collaborators were arrested, brought to Kielce, put on trial, convicted, and sentenced to prison.

A fortunate event happened on one of my trips out to the villages. In Busko Sdroi, someone, probably a German or a Volksdeutscher, had left behind a brand-new Opel Olympia and an NSU motorcycle. The villagers told us to take the vehicles, so we did. I reported the find to the head of the department in Kielce, and he told me to keep the car and motorcycle. When I told him that I could drive a motorcycle—I had learned how in Lubartow—but didn't know how to drive a car, he told me to find myself a chauffeur. So I did, and used the car for both business and pleasure. I kept the motorcycle too.

While I was working in Pinczow, two Polish men from Katowice walked for several days to report the murder of one of their sisters. She had been killed by a Volksdeutscher named Prosz, who was responsible for the deaths of many other Jews during the Occupation. With the German retreat, Prosz fled the town he had been living in, and our two Polish informants had tracked him down to where he was hiding, in his family's village near Pinczow.

I asked them to make an official report, testifying to all that they had told me. Then I asked if they would go with the police to identify Prosz. They agreed to do so. When the police brought him in, we interrogated him and he admitted the murders he had committed. We did not have to pass judgment ourselves, as we were now part of a government with a judicial system in which murderers of Jews could actually be brought to justice. It felt like a new world. The man was arrested and sent to Kielce, where he was tried and convicted; he died in prison.

Civilians helped us find many collaborators, including, in some cases, relatives or friends. As we had discovered before, as partisans, not all collaborators were equally guilty. Some people became collaborators for money or because they hated Jews, while others had been forced to collaborate by threats that failure to name names would result in the death of an imprisoned family member. We never punished people who had been put in that position.

One day, two Jewish sisters who had been hidden and saved by a gentile family walked into our office in Pinczow. They said that they were sharing quarters with two older men, also Jewish survivors. They wanted me to help them regain possession of the brewery their family had owned before the war. They were both in their twenties, shabbily dressed, obviously malnourished, and very distraught. They relaxed somewhat when I told them that I was also a Jew. I said that I could arrange for them to recover the brewery if they could show proof of ownership, but I advised them against doing business or living in Pinczow; anti-Semitism would pose a constant danger. The sisters listened carefully and said that they would need time to think things over. I gave them money and some goods we had confiscated from German warehouses and sent young Szymek along with them to see how they lived. Eventually, he became my liaison to them. They sent me homemade sponge cakes to show their gratitude, and one day, they invited me to their home for dinner.

I found them living in wretched conditions—no electricity, no facilities, just candles for light. The shadows they cast made the place even more depressing. The sight of those young women living in such misery moved me deeply, for, again, I couldn't help but think of my sisters. I strongly urged them to move to a bigger city, and to do so as soon as possible. They did. They moved to Lodz, where one of them married the owner of a leather-goods factory. When I went to Lodz a year later, the couple invited me to their home—a beautiful, warm, well-furnished apartment. They threw a big party for me as a way of thanking me for persuading the sisters to leave a city where they would almost certainly have been killed. They wined and dined me. In fact, I drank so much that I had to spend the night there. It was a night of joy. To be able to help these sisters have a better life filled me with pride.

In March 1945, I was transferred from Pinczow back to Kielce. I had asked young Szymek to accompany me, but he said that he didn't want to. Now that he was armed, he thought he was invincible. Several weeks later, a fascist group rampaged through Pinczow, released prisoners from the local jails, and killed several policemen. One of them was Szymek.

Sever Rubinstein, who had been assigned to the Kielce police department—not the Security Police—was at this time living by himself in an apartment allotted to him by the police department. He would often have his clothes cleaned at a laundry that a Polish woman operated out of her home. One day, wearing civilian clothes, he came in to pick up his laundry and found two men he had never seen before waiting for him in her apartment. They started questioning him: "Who are you? Where are you from?" and so on. Thinking that they were from the AK and fearing for his life, Sever drew his revolver. In the ensuing tussle, he hit one of the men with the butt of his gun. The two men grabbed him, arrested him, and took him for questioning to the headquarters of the Security Police, where he was savagely beaten.

Though I was working in the building, I didn't see Sever being brought in and learned only later that an AK man had been arrested. I went to check him out and found that the suspect was Sever. I immediately told the others that he was not AK but a comrade of mine from the partisans and a policeman besides, and they released him. He was in pretty bad shape. I cleaned him up and took care of him and suggested that he move in with me. There was room for two.

On May 8, we learned by radio that the war in Europe was over: Germany had surrendered. I cannot express the feelings that came over me when I heard the news. It wasn't happiness, because my thoughts were of my parents, of the loss of my family. I was overcome by grief. There was no mother or father, brother or sister with whom I could celebrate the end of the war. And I knew that in Poland, even after all the suffering of war, it was still dangerous to be a Jew.

IN JUNE, SEVER'S SISTER, Blimka, and Cesia Pomeranc came to Kielce. The two had become close friends during their time together in the forest. They stayed with us for two weeks and we showed them a good time. I took Cesia to the officers' ball a couple of times. On one of those occasions, Cesia and I were waltzing in a dance contest when a Russian captain cut in. I couldn't refuse. He told her to hang on, and she did as he whirled her across the floor. They won the first prize—a bottle of champagne, which we drank immediately—and everyone was happy.

One day, Cesia opened up to me in a way that she had never done before. She told me that in Lublin more than one member of our partisan group had asked for her hand in marriage. She had turned them down, she said, because she couldn't get me out of her mind. By that time, I was certain that I was the only member of my family left alive, and I recalled the advice of the elderly Jewish woman in Lubartow. I knew that I had to start a family of my own. I also knew that, of all the women I had known until this time, none of them compared to Cesia. I had learned, under the most extreme circumstances, what she was like, how gentle she was, how thoughtful and modest and courageous. I remember that Eisenberg said to me once, "Did you ever see such a special, pure girl? She is unbelievable!" She had earned the respect of every partisan in our group. I knew Cesia had been brought up in a fine family, with deep, traditional Jewish values. With Cesia, I felt completely at home. Even her delicious cooking tasted like my mother's. So after she told me about the proposals she had received, I agreed that we were meant to be together. She suggested that we marry, but I said that I wanted to wait until I was out of the military. I needed to be free and independent.

In the meantime, both she and Blimka had to return to

Lublin, so I took them to the train station. In those days, trains did not run according to any schedule; they came when they came and left when they left. I had things to do, so I kept leaving and coming back to the station to see if they had gone or were still where I had left them. After they had waited for more than four hours, I suggested that they come back to the apartment and try again the next day. That sounded like a good idea to them, so I told them to wait at the station while I hired a horse and carriage to take them and their luggage back to the apartment.

I rode off on my motorcycle, hired a horse and carriage, rode back to the station, and locked my motorcycle. When the carriage arrived, two drunken Russian officers—one a captain, the other a sergeant carrying a heavy knapsack—tried to take the carriage away from me. I told the captain, in Russian, that I had hired it; it was already spoken for.

He looked at me, saw that I was an officer, and said, "Okay, take it." I told the driver to pull up to the curb and went in to get Cesia and Blimka. When I came out, the two Russians were trying to steal my motorcycle, but couldn't because it was locked. A large crowd of Poles, including a number of army officers, had gathered to watch.

I walked over and asked the Russians what they were doing. They paid no attention. So after asking the Polish Army officers to keep the Russians from stealing my motorcycle, I went into the station to talk to a Russian major I had seen. He suggested that I bring the men inside to talk to him or shoot them like dogs in the street.

As usual, I had my Luger with me, and I walked back to the men, pointed my gun, and said, "Let's go see the major." Suddenly, the two drunks were sober. "Comrade," they cried, "we are Communists." As the onlookers moved in closer, the men slipped into the crowd and disappeared.

IN JUNE, THE HEAD OF THE SECURITY POLICE in the state of Kielce summoned me to his office. My mission was an urgent one, he said. I was given two letters to deliver: one to the head of the Security Police in Skarzysk, a town some one hundred kilometers away, the other to the head of the Skarzysk police. The letters instructed them to give me all the assistance I might need to carry out my assignment and informed them that I was in charge of the operation. A group of Polish officers occupying an entire train car—whose number I was given—would be arriving in Skarzysk from Katowice. I was to arrest them all, and I should enlist all the manpower available from the two departments to assist me in this arrest. When the mission was completed, I was to call Kielce immediately.

There was no time to lose. I was ordered to leave, by car, immediately. I was not told the reason for the arrest, and, upon arriving at the station, I refrained from making the arrests myself, instructing the other officers to make them. As an officer myself, I felt uncomfortable being in charge of an operation that called for the arrest of other officers. There were maybe altogether eight or ten of them, ranging in rank from major to sergeant, and including two or three women in uniform. The arrests went off smoothly, and I made the call to Kielce, informing them that the mission had been accomplished. I was told to remain and await the arrival of the Kielce police. When they arrived, one of the officers noticed that the captain, though disarmed, was still wearing his belt. I was given hell for this: the captain could have used his belt to commit suicide. The group was loaded onto a Russian truck and taken away to Kielce.

Later, I learned that the Security Police had received information that the officers were part of the fascist opposition. They had secured forged passes that allowed them to travel to Lublin for vacation, when, in fact, their intention was to organize an insurgency against the government. I suspected that I had been entrusted with this mission because my superiors knew that, as a Jew, I would be unlikely to have any allegiance to or connections with any fascist group. I could be trusted.

As the days wore on, I began to think about my future with Cesia, and I could not think of any reason for the two of us to remain in Poland. As part of my job, I had interviewed many Poles who, unaware that I was a Jew, made no attempt to conceal their feelings about Jews. As a result, I had come to realize the depth of Polish anti-Semitism. It was frightening. In my job, I read many official reports of fascist gangs riding the trains in search of Jewish survivors. In some instances, the Jews were harassed; in others, they were thrown off trains moving at high speed. I heard the news of my fellow comrade Jusek, who returned to his hometown of Bystrzejowice only to be murdered when fascist thugs threw a grenade into his home while he was sleeping. I knew that, because of the shortage of manpower in the branches of the new Polish government, especially in the areas of security and policing, fascist elements were easily able to infiltrate these institutions. Reports about the harassment or murder of Jews were seldom followed up.

All during the war, and after the war, even when I had a gun and was wearing my uniform, I was worried that I could be shot or arrested at any time, just for being a Jew. At first, I felt somewhat secure as I walked the streets in my Polish officer's uniform, but news spread that Jews in the police had also been threatened and murdered. So I had no illusions. I felt that I could be killed at any time. Later, we learned of a massacre of forty-three Jews in the very town in which we were living and working, Kielce; this happened a month after we left. Of course, there were decent Poles, both in the rabidly anti-Semitic Kielce area and throughout the country, but they were a minority. Finally, I did not see a rosy future for Jews in Poland. I knew that Cesia and I would want to raise our children with Torah, in a traditional Jewish home as part of a community of Jews. As I looked around, I began to see the tragedy that was Poland: a huge cemetery of our people, traditions, and culture.

I went to Korcinzki, who headed my department in Kielce, and requested a discharge. I told him I had some stomach problems that needed looking after and that I had been diagnosed with an ulcer. I also wanted to make one more search for any members of my family who might still be alive. Korcinzki replied, "I'm sorry, but I can't release you, because you're an officer. You'll have to go to Warsaw to request a discharge."

I asked him to give me a letter addressed to the head of the Security Police recommending my discharge for reasons of health. Ten minutes later, I picked up the letter and found a horse and carriage to take me to the airport. This was not a major airport but a grassland field that accommodated small Russian planes. I found a Russian pilot who was preparing to fly to Warsaw and willing to take me along in exchange for a bottle of vodka.

I was wearing an officer's uniform with a matching raincoat and carrying a pistol, which he told me to give him until the end of the flight, as passengers were forbidden to carry firearms. The plane was a two-seater with an open cockpit. I climbed into the seat behind the pilot. It was just a piece of plywood. I had to hold on when he banked, and I could feel the plywood starting to crack.

By the time we landed in Warsaw, I was feeling nauseated. The pilot returned my pistol, and I gave him enough money to buy a bottle of vodka, and then lay down on the grass, hoping the nausea would pass. When I got up, I took a carriage into the city and found a hotel room.

The next morning, I went to the government ministry and handed Korcinzki's letter to the bureaucrat it was addressed to. For the next ten days, I was sent to several clinics for examinations to determine the cause of my stomach troubles. I had a good idea what the cause was. Unhappy with my job and eager to get out, I had been drinking too much. If that's all they could find that was wrong with me, I realized, I probably wouldn't get my discharge papers. Luckily for me, the problem was diagnosed as an inflammation of mucus membranes in my intestines, which sounded serious. I was given a sealed envelope that I was to give to my superiors when I returned to Kielce.

One afternoon, between visits to doctors' offices, I stretched out on the banks of the Vistula River to sunbathe in my bathing suit. I fell asleep. When I woke up, I felt queasy and dove into the water for a swim. When I tried to climb back on shore, it was a real struggle. Everything hurt. Then I saw why: I was badly sunburned. My chest and legs were red and swollen. I was unable to get dressed, except for my pants. When I tried to button my jacket, I found that I couldn't: it was too painful. I covered myself with the sleeveless officer's raincoat so that I wouldn't look like a bum.

Seeing a building farther down along the riverbank, I stumbled toward it and asked the janitor if I could sleep there. He went inside and a minute later out came a nun, the mother superior. She told me that men weren't allowed to sleep at the convent. Judging by the way she looked at me, I think she thought I was a deserter.

I started to move down the embankment when a young woman came running after me. "Mr. Lieutenant," she called out, and then offered to help me. Her apartment was nearby, she said; I could rest there, if I needed to. I said I would like that, and she took me to a tiny room with a bed. I lay down and immediately fell asleep. When she looked in on me the next morning, I was unable to move. She helped me dress and offered to put me in touch with "the right people." I had the feeling that something was wrong here: who were these "right people"? I sensed that she meant anti-government people—fascists. So I gave her the money she needed to get my breakfast, and as soon as she had gone, I chased after a streetcar, jumped on, and returned to my hotel. There the maid applied cold fresh-cream compresses on my sunburned skin. It was like putting an iron on a wet towel. My skin steamed.

When I returned to Kielce, I presented the sealed envelope I had picked up in Warsaw and was discharged. For reasons that were never explained to me, I would be allowed to continue to wear my uniform and carry my pistol. The colleagues in my department, 10 or 15 percent of them Jews, thought I was crazy. How could I leave a job like this, with a chauffeured car, a motorcycle, and an apartment, and with no clue as to how I was going to make a living? But my mind was made up. Since I was not asked to return my uniform or pistol, I continued to wear them; they might help open doors that would otherwise be closed. Besides, I was proud of the rank and status that I had achieved.

After my discharge, I went to Kraków with Sever Rubinstein. We met up with Loterstein, Finkel, and Eisenberg. I told them about my plans and they said they had the same idea. Sever and I went on to Breslau to visit Gruber. The city had been heavily bombed. The scene was chaotic: abandoned shops and stores, factories being looted, people loading up on sugar, furs, and every conceivable kind of merchandise from places that had been under German control. There was a police department, and Sam Gruber was the head of it, but, as elsewhere in Poland, the department was understaffed and powerless to control the looting.

We were reunited with Sam and his wife, Krisha, at their home. Sam was a father by this time—a family man. We had a *l'chaim*, reminisced, and told him of our plans to leave Poland. He, too, had been thinking of leaving.

When we returned to Lublin, I helped Cesia pack her few belongings, after which we traveled together to Lubartow to visit the Tunkelschwartzes. When we told them that we were engaged, they immediately offered to hold the wedding in their home.

I insisted on paying for the wedding, so I needed money. I tried my luck as a dealer in whatever produce I could find a market for. First, I went to a butcher shop and bought fifty kilos of raw meat fat. Then Cesia and I brought the fat by train to the city of Koshalin; we went straight to the market and traded it for four Singer sewing machines—a rare and needed commodity in Lublin—and a bit of money. If we had been more experienced at this, we might have traded the meat for diamonds, as others did, but we were happy with the deal we made and to wind up with some cash in our pockets.

Cesia and I headed back to Lubartow by train. There was a stopover in Bidgoszcz, where we had to wait a few hours for the connection to Lublin. We checked our luggage at the station and walked over to the city's main park. We were sitting on a bench, enjoying the beautiful day, when a gypsy came over and offered to read my palm. I tried to shoo her away, but she grabbed my hand, so I said, "Oh, all right. Go ahead. Read my fortune."

She studied my palm and said, "You are going on a long journey. You will have two children, and you will be successful and happy."

I just laughed. I was in uniform and we had no luggage with us. How could she possibly know our plans? But she was right, even down to the number of children we would have.

On returning to Lubartow, I quickly sold the sewing machines and made enough money to pay for our wedding—the food, the drink, and the music. We chose September 6 as the date and invited all of our friends in Lublin to celebrate with us. We also invited many of my former colleagues from the Security Police and the Russian Army. Some of them made sure that the neighborhood was secure, and that no Jew haters would spoil the festivities. Cesia's three brothers—Jurek, Janek, and Abie—arrived from Lublin.

The Tunkelschwartzes prepared everything. They cooked and baked all of our favorite Jewish dishes and cakes. We had decided to do everything as traditionally as possible. Somehow, Cesia managed to find a wedding gown, and Blimka brought a white veil from Lublin. The chuppah, the marriage canopy, was made out of a *tallis*, a prayer shawl, that belonged to Berek. A Jewish survivor who claimed to be a rabbi was asked to perform the ceremony. Normally, the mother of the bride and the mother of the groom walk the bride to the chuppah, holding lighted candles. We asked Blimka and Mrs. Tunkelschwartz to stand in for our beloved mothers. However, we were all in for a surprise. As Cesia began to walk down the aisle, with Blimka and Mrs. Tunkelschwartz on either side holding the candles, a Russian captain scooped her up and deposited her under the chuppah, right next to me. No one tried to stop him because he was so drunk. At the end of the ceremony, in Jewish tradition, I stomped on the wineglass and we were married. Klezmer musicians played and the vodka flowed like water. Everyone ate and drank and drank and ate and sang. We even danced, though there wasn't much room for dancing. The party lasted for three days. Our guests slept as many as four to a bed, on the floor, wherever they could find a place, then awoke and began to party again. Fortunately, someone had a camera. Cesia and I posed in the street in front of the house for a wedding portrait with her three brothers—our only family members there. These photos are part of my most treasured possessions.

A few days after the party, Cesia and I left for Stettin, near the new German border, a strategic location for Jews trying to get out of Poland. Cesia's brother Janek, who lived in Stettin, found us an apartment. She also had a cousin there, Joseph Glinzman, a butcher who had taken over an empty butcher shop and bought cattle and sold meat.

One morning, I went to the Russian authorities in town and asked them for a pass to Berlin; I said that I wanted to look for my family. Because I was in uniform, they asked no questions and issued the pass. Leaving Cesia in Stettin, I went to Berlin, to the Russian zone, to the office of the American Jewish Joint

Distribution Committee, or the Joint, for short, on Oranien-burgerstrasse, where displaced persons could apply for assistance. There I was told that there were two DP, or displaced person, camps in the American zone: one at Schlachtensee, the other at Tempelhof. There were many other such camps throughout Germany in the different Allied zones, but our goal was to be with the Americans.

When I returned to Stettin, I told Cesia and her brothers about the DP camps and how we could apply. In the meantime, we had settled into an apartment that belonged to a German woman who served as our maid. There were no kosher restaurants in town, so Cesia ended up cooking meals for at least fifteen of our friends every day. They were like family.

Aron Gotz, one of Gruber's men, who had been the cook for our troops and in whose soup we once found a rag, was working in the Stettin police department. He met a woman named Regina, a beautiful blonde, and wanted to marry her. My brother-in-law Janek and I made them a wedding in Aron's apartment, with meat provided by Cesia's cousin, cases of vodka, and a musician. Some Russian soldiers on patrol passed by and, hearing the music, crashed the party. We fed them and gave them plenty of vodka, but when they left, they took our bicycles, which we kept outside in the hallway. The behavior of the Russians was completely unpredictable; some were very nice, very helpful, but there were also those who took Jewish women who had survived the death camps and turned them into sex slaves in their barracks. They terrorized the women by telling them that, since they had survived, they were probably spies and deserved whatever punishment the Russians felt like meting out. Five of these women, in their mid-twenties, managed to escape, and they were the ones who told me what was happening.

We put these women in contact with some *landsmen* (Jews from the same area they came from), who in turn led them to the Bricha (Hebrew for "escape"), the network that organized the clandestine movement of Jews out of Poland and into the U.S.-occupied zone of Germany, and from there to Palestine.

One rainy afternoon, Gotz and I were walking down a street when a Polish police officer stopped us and demanded to see our papers. Gotz was wearing his police uniform, but he wasn't an officer; I was wearing mine, but it was concealed by my rain cape, so the Pole couldn't see that I was an officer. Knowing the rules, I demanded to see his papers. First, he started to mumble; then he began making anti-Semitic remarks about Gotz. This made me furious. I pulled out my Luger and pistol-whipped him twice across the face. As a crowd gathered, a German woman ran out of the building and told us that this police officer's buddy was upstairs, stealing Persian carpets. The thief got away, but we tied up the policeman, took him down to the police station, and pressed charges, and he was arrested.

Cesia and I spent a lot of time trying to figure out how to get out of Poland. We knew that it was impossible to do so legally. We had to find a way to smuggle ourselves across the border and into Berlin. I was always putting out feelers, trying to pick up information about means of escape. Then one day,

I was introduced to a Russian driver who carried Russian Army mail from Stettin to Berlin, a distance of about two hundred kilometers. He was smuggling people, for a price, across the border, along with the mail. When we met with him, we set a date and made arrangements for payment. We handed over our apartment, along with our belongings, for safekeeping, to a cousin of Cesia's who had survived the war in Russia.

We left with nothing but the clothes on our backs and an extra set of underwear. I wore a civilian suit that I had a Jewish tailor make up for me in Kielce so I could shed my officer's uniform. The Russian parked on a prearranged side street and was waiting for us at the appointed time. After we paid him, he opened the back of the van and we jumped in. We lay down and he piled the mailbags all around us. As he took off, we wondered what would happen when we got to the Russian checkpoint. But nothing happened. The patrol just waved the driver through. When we arrived at Oranienburg-erstrasse, the Russian pulled over, opened the side door, and let us out. We gave him a tip, enough for a couple of bottles of vodka. We were now free Jews in Berlin, in the Russian zone. We had passed another milestone in our lives. We entered the offices of the Joint and were quickly assigned to the DP camp in Schlachtensee in the American zone.

Schlachtensee was a huge transit camp, from which displaced persons were sent to other camps in the Allied zone. There were thousands of Jews there. I was now among my people. I would no longer have to look over my shoulder, no longer have to worry about what might happen to Cesia or to me. Now, in Germany, the feeling I had was completely different. Even though I hated the Germans, I felt free.

We were assigned to what had been German Army barracks, where there were beds and facilities. We walked around a little square there and ate in the cafeteria. We met up with friends and with Cesia's cousin Glinzman. After spending a few days at the Schlachtensee camp, we were moved on to a second camp, also in the American zone, and then to a third, in Zeilsheim. Zeilsheim was a small, lovely village, on the outskirts of Frankfurt. The Americans had resettled German residents and placed refugees in what was good housing—regular homes. We were eager to move in but had to wait our turn for a house, so in the meantime, we rented a room in a house right behind the camp.

One of the people who passed through the camp was Sam Gruber. He told us an amazing tale. He had learned that the AK planned to assassinate him because he was a Jew who held an important position, but an informant inside the AK had tipped him off, saying that as a Jew himself, he couldn't allow him to be killed. He also warned Gruber that, if he wanted to live, he should leave Poland at once—so now there he was in Zeilsheim with his family. Later, Gruber left to teach at a Jewish children's refugee camp in Bavaria.

Once we were settled in Zeilsheim, I decided to go back to Poland to see if I could get my cousin Froim out of the country. I covered my expenses by dealing in leather—buying a bundle in Stuttgart, a center for the tanning trade, and selling it in Poland. I found Froim in Katowice and urged him to come with me into the free world. But by now he had a gentile girlfriend and was enjoying his life. He told me that Shlomo Morel, Yitzchak's younger brother and another comrade of ours, also felt settled there, so neither of them wanted to leave. I was disappointed and frustrated that Froim would not listen to me. We had survived so much together, had endured so many hardships together, especially when he was wounded, and somehow I had the feeling that one day he would regret this decision.

Froim and Shlomo were exceptions. The great majority of the Jews I knew left Poland. Most went to Palestine, the rest to Australia, South America, and the United States.

Back in Zeilsheim, I was soon involved in the black market, like everyone else who wanted to earn a living. American Jewish soldiers and relief workers used to come to the camps to hear the stories of the survivors, and they brought us all sorts of goods you couldn't find in German stores—chocolate, cigarettes, silk and nylon stockings, margarine, coffee, whiskey. Some of us made deals with them to bring larger quantities of goods that we could sell, and so, slowly but surely, each of us began finding customers.

The soldiers also put us in touch with people who could ship in truckloads and railroad carloads of goods. I had struck up an acquaintance with a German Jew named Levy, who had somehow "organized" a Volkswagen. He introduced me to people who ran a Belgian import-export company that the Germans had taken over and that the family had now reclaimed. They had warehouses and trucks and everything we needed to bring in goods. It wasn't long before I became one of their top traders. We sold tons of coffee beans to people who would roast it, and truckloads of margarine, chocolate, and cigarettes.

A FEW MONTHS AFTER WE ARRIVED in Zeilsheim, the Joint asked us to which country we would like to emigrate. At about the same time, an American from Chicago named Blumenkrantz showed up in Zeilsheim and sent me regards from my uncles Avrum and Noach Blackman. I had always known that I had uncles in Chicago because they used to write letters to my parents. But until this man appeared, I didn't know how to find them. Blumenkrantz told me that my uncles were searching for relatives and had managed to find two. One was my first cousin Shmuel Blajchman, who had left Kamionka early on for Russia and was now living in Schleswig-Holstein, in the British zone. The other was me. Blumenkrantz reported back to Chicago that both of us had been found, and I soon received letters from my uncles, and a correspondence between us began.

In Zeilsheim, I accidentally found another first cousin, Sarah Gritzmacher, the daughter of my mother's sister. Sarah, who had been raised in Kotzk, had managed to escape Poland in 1942. She survived in Germany with two friends—Chanka and Stasha—by posing as Polish gentiles, with forged papers. The three women worked in a factory throughout the war. Sarah and I were thrilled to find each other. She had met and married a man named Moniek Stawski, in Zeilsheim. Moniek was a wheeler-dealer who bought used cars, mostly Mercedes, fixed them up, and resold them at a big markup. When the camp in Zeilsheim was closed, in 1948, all of us moved to Frankfurt, where Moniek opened a coffee-bean roasting company, with the help of Levy, who found us an apartment and another for Moniek. We took a three-bedroom apartment. We gave David Rubinstein, Sever's brother, and his wife, Bella, the largest bedroom because they had a baby. Cesia and I took the second, smaller bedroom, and kept the third, tiny bedroom for anyone who needed a place to stay.

My good friend Marion Dworecki married Blimka Rubinstein and moved into the same building, a few floors above us. We went everywhere together; we marketed, cooked, and ate in each other's homes, and dreamed of our futures together. We began to attend the Frankfurt synagogue every Saturday, and life slowly began to feel normal. Cesia's brothers came to join us, and it was not unusual to find fifteen or so people eating dinner in our home. Abie, with strong Zionist yearnings, emigrated to Israel with the Children's Aliyah. Sever, who had married a widow named Lily Botnik, found an apartment in a nearby neighborhood, as did the Stawskis. So we had our own small community of friends.

One Sunday, a German with whom Dworecki, Sever, and David were doing business invited them to take a ride with him around Frankfurt. Later, Cesia and I wondered if Dworecki had a premonition that something was going to happen, because he came down to our apartment at least three times that day to urge me to come along. But I said no thanks.

I didn't know the German and I didn't feel like going. Blimka, who was pregnant, David, Bella, and baby Jackie all went along for this ride. Half an hour later, we heard that there had been an accident. The drunk driver of a Coca-Cola truck had rammed the car. Dworecki was killed instantly. Blimka's hips were broken and she lost the baby she was carrying. David and Bella were injured, and Jackie, about eighteen months old, was thrown through the windshield, but he survived unharmed. We took him home and cared for him while his parents and Blimka recuperated in the hospital. Blimka was completely distraught and in a state of shock. She and Dworecki had been very much in love; they had survived at each other's side and were looking forward to life and a new baby.

As for me, I couldn't believe it. My friend Dworecki, the daring demolition expert, had survived the war only to be killed on a leisurely Sunday afternoon outing. For days I wasn't myself. Dworecki had been a great partisan, a very close and dear friend. We had gone through so much together, and to have him die in a senseless accident, just as he was starting a new life, was devastating.

The behavior of the German who invited us all to go on that Sunday drive was typical of the change that had come over the Germans. Now that they needed Jews like us who could help them obtain the basic necessities, they were very polite. If they hated us, they did not show it. The difference in attitude between Poles and Germans toward the Jews was the difference between day and night. Hatred never died with the Poles, who wanted us out of the country altogether, or dead.

Cesia and I lived in Frankfurt from 1948 until 1951, when we finally got our visas. We ate well, we slept well, we went to shul on *Shabbos,* kept a kosher home, and had lots of friends, so we felt like one big family. We became a real family on March 13, 1949, when Cesia gave birth to our first child, Bella Ita, who was named for her two grandmothers.

Two years later, in April 1951, we received a phone call from the Joint telling us, in Yiddish, "Mazel tov. You can come get your tickets to America."

I thanked the caller but told him that I could afford to pay my own way. We wanted to visit Israel first because Cesia's younger brother, Abie, was in a kibbutz there. He had served in the Israeli Army; we hoped to persuade him to come with us to America. Also, the trip would give us a chance to see what life was like in the Promised Land. We left Bella with a nursemaid and took a train to Zurich, where we caught a plane to Tel Aviv.

Before the war, Cesia's father had run a lumber business in the Wlodowa area and had a business partner named Schlachter. Schlachter escaped to Russia early in the war and served as a member of General Wladyslaw Anders's army of nearly one hundred and sixty thousand, mostly Poles captured and imprisoned by the Russians when the Soviet Union invaded Poland and then released when Germany attacked Russia.

These men refused to serve in the Russian Army, so Stalin came to an understanding with the Polish government-in-exile in London and agreed to support a Polish army with Anders as general in command. However, Stalin would not permit Anders to fight on the front against Germany, so Anders and his one hundred and fifty-nine thousand Poles were sent to Persia and Palestine for training. Schlachter was one of those troops; another was Menachem Begin, a veteran of the Free Polish Army and leader of the Irgun, who later became prime minister of Israel.

We met with Schlachter, who embraced us like his own children and gave us a tour of Jerusalem. It was through him that we met an Israeli rabbi and minister of some sort who took us out to dinner one night and who, when we told him we had a travel visa that we could use for America or Israel, said, "*Kinderlach*, my children, you have a visa for America. Israel is a hard life. Go to America, and you will have time to come back to Israel later."

We stayed in Israel for a month. Cesia was happy there, glad to be reunited with her family and our comrades in arms. Before we went back to Europe to leave for America, Cesia and I invited them all, about thirty comrades, to a celebration we arranged in Tel Aviv. We ate and drank far into the night, reliving old times.

In Frankfurt, we packed and bought tickets on the *Queen Elizabeth* to the United States for the three of us. We stayed a few weeks in Paris, and it was there that Cesia, who was about two months pregnant, lost the baby. We put off taking the train to Cherbourg to allow her time to recuperate. We almost waited too long. After checking out, we hailed a taxi, but the traffic was so heavy that we had to run for the train in the Gare du Nord, where Cesia's brother and comrades from the old days were waiting for us.

The rough crossing took five days. On the fifth day, when we came up on deck, we could see the Statue of Liberty and the Manhattan skyline. I had never seen photographs of the city, so the sight of those tall buildings was astonishing. As for the Statue of Liberty, I had no idea then what it stood for. This was my first look at America, the *goldene medina,* the land of gold. I found it hard to believe that we had really lived to see this day. Now we were going to make a fresh start, begin a new life. I made the blessing *Shehechaynu, Ve kimonu ve higyanu lasman ha zeh.* I thanked God that we had survived and come to this place in this time.

CHAPTER VII

RETURN TO POLAND

In 1985, I RETURNED to Poland. Cesia had given me the location where she had worked as a slave laborer in Adampol. I flew to Frankfurt, picked up my cousin Froim, and we flew to Warsaw, where I hired a car and driver. We found the place where my in-laws and so many others had been killed. A monument there commemorates the massacre of Polish citizens, but it makes no mention of Jews, even though all the people murdered were Jews. I asked a man if anyone was still around who remembered the event.

He told me to wait, and sent somebody off to look for a person who had been there at the time. We waited about half an hour. When nobody showed up, I told some boys who were hanging around to tell the man that I was willing to pay him. Soon a man came out of one of the houses. He looked about eighty, stooped and with wrinkled hands and face, but when

I asked him how old he was, he said that he was in his late fifties. I asked if he could tell us what he remembered about that day.

"All I know is they took the people from the laborers' camp and made them dig a ditch," he said. "Even people in the village had to help dig the ditch. Then they made the Jews walk into the ditch and shot them all. After the Germans left, a little boy crawled out of the ditch and walked into the forest."

I called Cesia in New York City and told her the story, and she said, "That was my brother Abie." Abie refused to go back to Poland because of his memories.

On that same trip, I went to Kamionka, but it was just a drive-through. I did not want to stop. The streets had been paved, and the town had its own water system, and our shul, which the Germans had desecrated and used as an office, was now the town hall. Then we went to the death camps—to Treblinka, Sobibor, Auschwitz, and Majdanek. It was to the camp at Majdanek that my family and the other Jews of Kamionka and the surrounding area were sent. The sight of these places left us speechless.

My Chicago cousin Al visited Kamionka in 1989. He went to the town hall to ask if they had any resident listing for Blajchman. They said, "Yes, Moishe Blajchman," and gave him the address: 10 Main Street. Moishe Blajchman was my cousin Shmuel's father. When Al got to the house, a woman opened the door. He asked, "What's your name?" And she said, "I'm the wife of Moishe Blajchman." He almost fainted.

Then he said that he was a cousin from Chicago, and she said that she and her husband had only recently moved in. Al listened to her story and then told her that his family name was Blajchman and that he knew there were no relatives still living in Kamionka. She turned white. It was obvious that Poles had moved into the confiscated properties vacated by the doomed Jews in 1942 and had never changed the names on the public rolls. So not only did a Polish family steal our property; it also stole the Blajchman name.

Cesia had never wanted to return to Poland, but in 1995 she did. First we went to Israel to attend a bar mitzvah. On the way home, we flew to Warsaw, then drove to Adampol, to the death camps, and to Wyryki, a village near Cesia's childhood home where her family used to go on summer holidays. Remarkably, some of the Poles there recognized and remembered her. One of the men we met had gone to school in Wlodowa-Wyryki with Cesia's brother Janek. We were amazed to see how poor the people were. They wanted to give us something to eat, even though they had nothing. We were carrying smoked turkey, bologna, all kinds of kosher foodstuffs from Israel, so we cut up several pounds of turkey and we all ate together. We did not talk about the war. Instead, Cesia and Janek's former schoolmate reminisced about life before the Germans came.

My nephews and our daughter, Bella, wanted to visit Auschwitz and I agreed to go with them, while Cesia, who did not want to see any more of the horrors of war, remained in Warsaw. We hired a car and driver and noticed that there were gas-station convenience stores along the highway. So we stopped at one to buy sodas. Everything was fine until my nephew Michael asked for a cheese sandwich, and the clerk pretended not to see us or hear us. So our Polish driver went in and bought the sandwich for us. There are no longer many Jews in Poland, but it is my personal belief that even the few who are there are still hated by most Poles.

As for the Poles who helped us during the war—people like the Dabrowskis and the Kloses—I will never forget their kindness, the way they risked their lives to help Jews in need.

In 1993, I received a letter from the Jewish Institute in Warsaw, asking if I knew anything about the incident involving the death of the good farmer Boleslaw Dabrowski. I confirmed what had happened forty years before and was pleased to be subsequently informed by Yad Vashem in Jerusalem that the honor of Righteous Among the Nations had been conferred upon Dabrowski for his selfless courage. In 1994, during a visit to Poland, I was able to find Wanda Dudek, who was by then living in Lublin. She did not immediately recognize me, and it took her sons some time to convince her that I was myself. I asked her if she would like to be listed among the Righteous Among the Nations, and she said no because she feared that the Jew haters in the region would find out and her sons would suffer as a result.

After I came to America, I tried to locate the Klos family, which had sheltered me during the early days following my escape from Kamionka. I sought them out through the Red Cross but got nowhere until I was helped by a Polish woman who had emigrated to Canada and was involved in identifying Poles who had saved Jewish lives. She contacted a priest in a community near Kamionka and learned that the name was spelled Klos, not Glos, as I had thought.

By then, the farmer and his wife were dead and the children's whereabouts unknown. I took the necessary steps, and in 1996, Alexsander and Alfreda Klos were listed among the Righteous Among the Nations honored at Yad Vashem in Israel.

Thinking of all those who died or were murdered—of Dabrowski and my friends and comrades, of my grandfather, my whole family, and millions of innocent others—I have often wondered why I survived when so many didn't. I have no answer. As a partisan, I was involved in many battles, with close fire coming at me from all sides. My friends and comrades, good men who had wanted nothing more than the opportunity to lead a simple life in the manner of their ancestors in Poland, died all around me. I think that I wasn't really afraid during those times, maybe because I never thought about dying or surviving at all. My focus was on what I could do at any given moment against the enemy. Revenge had become my way of life. And now, more than sixty years later, I feel that whatever I did to take revenge on the Germans and on their collaborators who rounded up and killed our families and friends, who had made war on the Jewish people, was not enough. I did the utmost that I could under the circumstances. At the same time, I tried never to harm an innocent person, because I did not believe in collective punishment—that if one German or Pole had behaved criminally, an innocent party should have to pay the penalty. That was the way the Nazis had behaved; it was not my way.

We were not ruthless and we were not reckless. We never went on a mission if we had no chance of survival. We never went against a tank unit, for example. Our intention was always to choose the job where the tactic was to hit and run.

Many times, as we moved about the forests, I would sense things—which path to take, where to go, when to stop moving and listen. I will never know what it was about the sight of the cross on the church spire in Lubartow that reminded me of my promise to myself not to go with the others but to go my own way, but if I had not received that sign, I would not have survived. Nor would I have survived if I had not happened to meet Mottele on that night in Kamionka and Chaim in the middle of the forest. These are mysteries I cannot explain.

A MEMORIAL TO ALL JEWISH FIGHTERS IN WORLD WAR II

IN THE 1960S, SAM GRUBER, Sever Rubinstein, Jack (Janek) Pomeranc, Sam Finkel, Isaak Mendelson, and I—all former partisans—created the Federation of Former Jewish Underground Fighters Against Nazism. The goal was to make people aware that not all Jews went to the slaughter like sheep, that many fought back against the Nazis and their collaborators and all the Polish fascist groups, who were as committed to our destruction as the Germans.

Sever was the president and Gruber was vice president. Sever was somehow able to get a senator from New York to put something about the partisans into the *Congressional Record*. For several years, our main activity consisted of holding fund-raising dinners for the Israel Defense Forces (IDF). By the 1980s, Sever had died; Gruber was president, and I was vice president.

It was in the 1980s, too, that I read Shmuel Krakowski's

The War of the Doomed, in which my name appeared in several places. I felt that the information about me and my unit was incomplete, and I became determined to tell our story in my own words. Also, it was in these years that the world gathering of survivors in Jerusalem was being planned. I thought the time had come to memorialize our comrades who fought and died during World War II.

I really did not know how to begin. On several visits to Israel, I shared my thoughts with old friends who said, "It's a good idea, Frank, but we can't do it in Israel because we have no money."

I got together with some of my old comrades in arms—Mikolai Berezin, Shlomo Eisenberg, and Gershon Silberman—and we exchanged ideas and started looking for a suitable place for such a memorial. They took me to a forest outside of Tel Aviv where people spent weekends and some had erected various forms of memorial stones. I said, "Look, this is not the place for our fallen comrades. Who comes here? We have to find a place where it's both peaceful and easily accessible to everyone."

Word spread that we were looking for a place and a way to create an appropriate memorial. A fellow from Tel Aviv named Weiselfish came to New York to see Gruber, whom he knew from the war. He had lost a leg in the war and claimed to have been a general in the Russian Army. The two had a serious talk and Weiselfish said that he could help find a place for the monument.

This was the first of several visits, and each time Weiselfish came to New York, I gave him a few hundred dollars. Finally, on one visit he told us he had found an ideal location: it was at an intersection on the main road connecting Tel Aviv, Haifa, and Jerusalem. I told him I needed to know if a monument could be built on that site. When he returned, all he brought were some sketches of an office building, which he wanted me to pay for. We could put the monument on the roof, he said.

"Do you take me for a fool?" I said. "You build yourself your office building, and I'll see if I want to put the monument on top of it." And that was the end of the story.

I continued to make known my intention to create a memorial, and the word spread. One of the people I spoke to was Eli Zborowski, whom I saw every Saturday at Temple Young Israel in Forest Hills. While they were reading the Torah, we used to talk about our past — Poles had killed his father, and Poles had also hidden him — and I told him that I had this stone on my heart: how to commemorate my comrades who had fallen in battle fighting against the Nazis and their collaborators and the Polish fascist groups.

Eli was sympathetic to my desire to create a monument, and one day he called me from the airport after returning from Israel. "Frank," he said, "I have something for you and I'll see you in shul." And at shul he told me that he had a commitment from Yad Vashem. "They will give us space on their grounds to build a monument."

I said, "I would like to have the commitment in writing. Then we can start raising funds."

The letter was sent to Sam Gruber, after which Eli and I

invited a group of people, many of them my friends, to work with us and contribute to the project. We created a committee to raise funds. In addition to Eli and me, we had Jack Pomeranc, William Mandel, Sam Skora, Israel Krakowski, Sam Bloch, Robert Born, Mark Palmer, and Joseph Holm, among others. Palmer worked really hard for us and was the one who went to Italy to get the Carrera marble for the monument. I want to take this opportunity, a once-in-a-lifetime chance, to publicly thank him in this book.

The result was the creation of the Committee to Erect a Monument to Partisans at Yad Vashem in Jerusalem. The committee determined that we should have a fund-raising luncheon and that I should be a guest of honor with Howard J. Samuels, former U.S. undersecretary of commerce, who had served as a lieutenant under General George S. Patton in the liberation of Jewish prisoners from the concentration camps. Samuels also held prominent positions with the Israel Bonds organization and with the American Jewish Congress. Air Force general Jerome Waldor attended the event in full uniform.

The inaugural luncheon took place on Sunday, September 16, 1984, at the Sheraton Centre in Manhattan. We collected more than a quarter of a million dollars from two hundred guests. Yad Vashem retained the sculptor Bernie Fink (who, coincidentally, was born the same year I entered the forest, 1942), and we chose a design from several that he had submitted. The final design consists of six hexagonal blocks of granite in two stacks of three, each block memorializing a million Jews killed in the

Holocaust, configured in such a way as to emphasize the shape of a Star of David in the open space at the center.

Many of the people who donated to the memorial were at the groundbreaking ceremony, and it took a full year before we could dedicate the monument to the Jewish soldiers and partisans on May 15, 1985. U.S. secretary of state George Schultz was in Israel at the time and was the first American official to place a wreath at our monument. I made one of the speeches on that afternoon. As of today, our memorial is the only monument that honors all Jews throughout the world who fought back against the Nazis.

My Address at the Unveiling of the
Jewish Fighters Monument at
Yad Vashem, Jerusalem
May 15, 1985

Ladies and gentlemen, fellow survivors, honored guests,

It is with great honor and deep satisfaction that I stand before you and this monument to our fallen Jewish fighters.

I and my wife, Cesia, who is here with me, are Holocaust survivors who survived as partisans fighting the enemy. We are gathered here today to dedicate this monument to the Jewish fighters who gave their lives in the struggle against the enemies of our people during World War II, the fallen partisans, ghetto fighters, and soldiers in all the Allied armies.

The fact that one and a half million Jews fought bravely against Nazi Germany and its satellites is too often ignored.

This is why this monument is so important as a reminder of this basic historical truth. Nowhere in the world is there a monument of this kind, dedicated especially to our Jewish fighters. We are here to remember their heroism; we are here to honor their memory.

Standing here as a former partisan, my thoughts go back to those days of struggle and combat. The memories of the past are hard to imagine, but then they were our reality and daily occupation. It was not merely a struggle for survival; history had placed on us the task of avenging the blood of our families and millions of our people brutally murdered by the Nazis.

I remember those comrades, the courageous, brave men and women who, together with us, answered the call of history: to defend Jewish lives, to defend Jewish honor and dignity. We are the fortunate ones; we are the survivors who must and will keep this legacy alive for generations to come.

I want to thank Yad Vashem for placing the monument on its sacred ground and to thank all of you here today for joining us in this ceremony. It gives me special pleasure to mention Dr. Yitzhak Arad, chairman of the Yad Vashem Directorate, and the entire Yad Vashem Council, who helped so much to create this monument; and my dear friend Eli Zborowski, the chairman of the International Society for Yad Vashem, without whom this monument may never have become reality; also, members of the monument committee (too many to be able to mention—please forgive me!); to my family, who gave me the encouragement to follow through on my convictions;

and lastly, to all friends who contributed funds and effort in building this monument.

As I stand in front of this Jewish Fighters Monument, I feel that my desire of many years has been fulfilled. I have always wanted to see a dignified memorial to all the Jewish fighting forces who participated in battles against Nazi Germany. Now we are privileged to have it unveiled for the world to see. As long as we live, as long as our children and our children's children live, we must meet at this monument and bring others to see it and to remember. Remember with sorrow and pride what has come before and how we as Jews survived the greatest tragedy that has ever befallen our people. Our hope is that one day soon, Jews of Israel and all over the world will live in peace, free of oppression, in a peaceful world.

Thank you.

HONOR ROLL OF PARTISAN FIGHTERS

These are the names that I remember. There are many more — perhaps two hundred — whose names I do not remember. FB

KAMIONKA GROUP

First Commander,
   Jankel Klerer
Second Commander,
   Frank Blaichman
Josef Hershman
Hershzel Herszman
Jusek Herzman
Leon Herzman
Max Jenier
Blimka Lamberg
Mendel Lamberg
Leble
Froim Lewin
Usher Lewin
Avram Reis
Esther Reis

Mosze Schneiderman
Shabse
Simcha
Fiszel Wacholder

MARKUSZOW GROUP

Joined with the Kamionka group in March 1943
Commander Isser Rosenberg
Wladek Edilstein
David Etinger
Atazs Fishbein
Chiel Gotlef
Ita Gotlef
Jusek
Mosze Kierszenbaum

Szmuel Laks
Wolve Laks
Chaia Loterstein
Michael Loterstein
Shlomo Morel
Yitzchak Morel
Moishe Peltz
Moishe Rok
Bella Rubinstein
Blimka Rubinstein
David Rubinstein
Sever Rubinstein
Tolka
Chanka Tomalewicz
Wladek Tomalewicz
Stefan Tuman
David Weingarten
Samuel Yeger

GRUBER GROUP

*Joined with the Kamionka/
Markuszow group in
June 1943*
Commander Sam Gruber
André
André
Mikolai Berezin
Marion Dworecki
Shlomo Eisenberg
Sam Finkel
Furman
Geniek

Aron Gotz
Geniek Lipman
Maczin
Matros
Jusek Pisacki
Romek
Wladek
Wladek

AL (PEOPLE'S ARMY)

*Assumed leadership of the
three united Jewish partisan
groups in June 1943*
General Mietek Moczar
General Rola-Zymierski
Brigadier Commander
    Alexander Skotnicki
Captain Jan
    Wojtovitcz
Captain Francziszek
    Volinski
Staszek Bialek
Pawel Dubek
Zib Fekvsz
Sidor Karziesz
Geniek Kaminsky
Stanislaw Jerzy Lec
Geniek Maksula
Leon Marzenta
Kolka Mieluch
Dr. Temczin
Wacek Wymolski

GRYNSZPAN GROUP

*Joined with other all-Jewish groups
in April 1944*
Commander Chiel Grynszpan
Henry Barbanel
Simcha Barbanel
Jurek Cholomsky
Dora
Roska Duman
David Fiedman
Adash Fiszbein
Abram Grispan
Leon Lerner
Pesel

Lonka Pfefferkorn
Avram Pomeranc
Cesia Pomeranc
Janek Pomeranc
Jurek Pomeranc
Joseph Rolnik
Abraham Rubinstein
David Rubinstein
Gershon Silberman
Tema
Harold Werner
Adam Winder
Lova Zicman

ACKNOWLEDGMENTS

I HAVE BEEN WANTING TO TELL this story for a long time. It's the story of what happened in those terrible days when Jews were hunted down and killed simply because they were Jews. It was also a time when Jewish partisans fought to defend themselves against their many enemies and avenge themselves on those who had taken their families to the death camps. I was a boy when I decided I would rather be killed trying to escape than wait to be taken. I am now eighty-four years old, and I am determined to keep alive the memory of those men and women, those who fought and those who died. It is important that those of us who fought and survived tell it the way it was.

When the war ended, we thought that Nazism, fascism, anti-Semitism, and racism were dead and gone forever. Now, so many years later, we see that they are alive and well and must still be combated.

I did not write this book alone. That would have been impossible. I didn't speak a word of English when I arrived in the United States, and learning to write in a new language is harder than learning to speak it. So I told my story to four people, over the course of several years. The first was Frances Kamien; next, Gordon Cohen; then Jeanette Friedman; and, finally, my daughter-in-law, Aviva Blaichman. Through the efforts of Sarah Lazin, a literary agent, I had the good fortune of meeting Jon Swan, whose talent, skills, and experience gave the text shape and flow. We have gone over my memoir for the past year. The process, in which my daughter-in-law has been the driving force, has taken much longer than either of us expected. As I read the transcripts, I kept feeling that things were missing—not just events and dates, but emotions that were often hard to express. As more and more memories returned, I did my best to inject the humor that sometimes occurs during difficult and traumatic times. It proved harder to describe the moments of grief and depression, and there were many of them.

I am grateful for all the help I received, but I am most grateful to my wife, Cesia; my daughter, Bella, and my son, Charles. Without their love, encouragement, and patience, I could not have seen my memoir through to completion.